MODERN FURNITURE CLASSICS

THAMES AND HUDSON

Charlotte Fiell and Peter Fiell

MODERN FURNITURE CLASSICS

SINCE 1945

347 illustrations, 144 in colour

For our daughter, Emelia Beatrice,
born while we were writing this book

p. 1 Exterior view of Fiell, 181
King's Road, London SW3

p. 3 André Dubreuil
Paris chair, 1988

Printed and bound in Japan by Dai
Nippon

Carlo Mollino
Chair for the Agra House, 1955

Frank Gehry
Imperial table, *c.* 1982

Gerrit Rietveld
Zig-zag chairs, 1934

Contents

1900 to 1945   Introduction: Ornament in exile

Josef Hoffmann
Sitzmaschine, 1908

Marcel Breuer
Wassily chair, 1925

Denham Maclaren
Glass and Zebra-skin chair,
1931

Frank Lloyd Wright
Chair designed for the
Kaufmann Department Store,
Pittsburgh, 1937

The term 'design' is used to describe a variety of components that have been subject to a creative process. Charles Eames interpreted design as 'a plan for arranging elements in such a way as to best accomplish a particular purpose'.[1] This is a classical definition of design and is necessarily rational. The rationalist design principles promoted by the Modern Movement represent the basis from which twentieth-century design has evolved.

A design that is highly rational in one period, however, may be considered anti-rational in another. Indeed, the history of furniture design in this century is dominated by two main themes: rationalism and anti-rationalism. Styling runs counter to design and can be regarded as essentially anti-rational. Functionalism and the industrial process are the primary concerns of design, whereas aesthetics are the central consideration of style. New styles are born out of the rejection of those that came before: Pop was in opposition to the 'good design' of the 1950s, High-Tech was a reaction to the anti-design of Pop and so forth.

Truly definitive or absolute design cannot be created because design is and always will be ephemeral. Although particular design solutions can only apply to specific purposes and periods in time, however, it is possible to speak in terms of 'classics'. Classic furniture is more forward-looking or better designed than its contemporaries. It represents a harmonic balancing of the objectives that characterize design and style, possesses an enduring aesthetic or functionalism and powerfully expresses the spirit of the time in which it was created.

Furniture designed after the Second World War bears the unmistakable mark of avant-garde design concepts formulated by the Modern Movement during the first half of the century. In order to understand the evolution of modernism and the development of contemporary design as we know it, however, one has to go even further back and examine what was happening during the last quarter of the nineteenth century, for it was then that the Arts and Crafts Movement was paving the way for modern design.

Rejecting the eclecticism and unashamed opulence of the High Victorian style, while renouncing the use of superfluous ornament as being symptomatic of a decadent society, the Arts and Crafts Movement turned towards a simpler and more rational code of design ethics. Arthur Heygate Mackmurdo (1851–1942), founder of the Century Guild, described the moral imperative felt by the Movement's leaders: 'The more extensive our vision, the more intensive our sentiment, the greater appears the human importance of this movement not as an aesthetic excursion; but as a mighty upheaval of man's spiritual nature.'[2]

Indeed, William Morris (1834–96), undoubtedly the Arts and Crafts Movement's greatest exponent, wished to reform the social order as well as attitudes to design. During the period that encompassed the High Victorian style, machine-made objects were often reproductions of handcrafted work and were therefore untruthful to the materials and the technology they employed. Morris & Co. favoured a return to traditional craftsmanship in which a guild system could operate, retailing designs that were inspired by traditional vernacular design formats and especially by medievalism. For all their apparent simplicity, designs such as the Sussex chair were, ironically, well beyond the means of many ordinary people, for much of their construction was done by hand. Morris condemned the cluttered living spaces of the High Victorian period, extolling people to 'have nothing in your house that you do not know to be useful or believe to be beautiful'.[3] His ideas were hugely influential on the Continent, and shops opened in Munich, Liège and Paris to sell the new furniture. In America, meanwhile, a version of Englishman Charles Eastlake's *Hints on Household Taste* was published in 1872 and was a tremendous popular success, introducing the views of the Arts and Crafts Movement to a market that had been preoccupied with the mass production of elaborate upholstered furniture. The Arts and Crafts Movement's distrust of hackneyed ornament and 'gadgetry' prompted the search for a new idealism in design that laid the ground for the Glasgow School, the Wiener Werkstätte and the work of American architect Frank Lloyd Wright (1867–1959), all of which were profoundly instrumental in the conception of the Modern Movement.

The work of the Glasgow School, particularly that of Charles Rennie Mackintosh (1868–1928), was to forge a link between the new aesthetics of the Arts and Crafts Movement and parallel developments on the Continent. Mackintosh's work was startlingly avant-garde in its day, for although the influence of the Arts and Crafts Movement is clear – he rejected worn-out historicism, insisting on careful use of ornament and genuine craftsmanship – his designs contain the curving organic elements of Art Nouveau, Celtic motifs from his native Scotland and curiously elongated forms. In his later designs Mackintosh employed geometric and abstract forms of ornament, at a time when non-representational art was only just beginning to emerge.

At the same time, in Vienna, the architect and designer Josef Hoffmann (1870–1956) was designing plain, linear furniture and interiors for the Wiener Werkstätte. It is important to remember that the furniture designs of Mackintosh, Hoffmann and others were only a small part of larger decorative schemes, for it was not until after the Second World War that 'designer' furniture was to take on a truly separate identity from the architecture surrounding it. The display of Mackintosh's furniture and interiors at the Vienna Secession exhibition of 1900 had a profound influence on the work of the Wiener Werkstätte; indeed, Franz Wärndörfer, who financially supported the Werkstätte, is thought to have bought some of Mackintosh's furniture for his dining-room, and Hoffmann visited Mackintosh in Scotland. Founded in 1903, the Werkstätte was a guild of designers engaged in all aspects of design, from textiles and graphics to furniture and metalwork; Wärndörfer had been impressed by the work of the British Guild of Handicraft founded by C.R. Ashbee (1863–1942). Hoffmann, nicknamed 'Quadratl' owing to his use of rectilinear forms, and his colleague Koloman Moser (1868–1918), also echoed the aims of the Arts and Crafts Movement – and perhaps recalled the simple honesty of Biedermeier furniture, which had been submerged by ostentatious historicism – when they stated in 1905 that for the Wiener Werkstätte the 'guiding principle is function, utility our first condition, and our strength must lie in good proportions and the proper treatment of material. We shall seek to decorate when it seems required but we do not feel obliged to adorn at any price'.[4] The Hoffmann Sitzmaschine, a reclining chair designed in 1908, certainly meets the Werkstätte's criterion of minimal ornament. It was originally sold with or without large horsehair-filled, upholstered cushions. More often than not, the chair was purchased without the cushions, which may indicate, ironically, that the Sitzmaschine was acquired purely for its aesthetic appeal rather than for its function.

Walter Gropius (1883–1969) believed the later Bauhaus approach to design was the logical progression of ideas founded by the Deutscher Werkbund, of which Hoffmann was a member. The Deutscher Werkbund, founded in 1907, was set up, like the Wiener Werkstätte, in opposition to the decorative excesses of the then prevalent Art Nouveau style, or 'Jugendstil' as it was known in Germany. One of its members, Adolf Loos (1870–1933), wrote a paper in 1908 entitled *Ornament und Verbrechen (Ornament and Crime)*, in which he put forward the idea that excessive ornament could lead to the debasing of society and ultimately to crime. A later Werkbund publication, *Form ohne Ornament (Form without Ornament)*, of 1924, illustrated and expressed the virtues of plainer, more rationally based industrial designs. The movement aimed to promote closer co-operation between artists, architects and manufacturers, believing that the machine was not responsible for poor

design, but that designers had not ascertained how to use the machine to its maximum efficiency in aesthetic terms.

The question of mechanization versus handcrafted techniques was a long-running dispute. While William Morris had been fervently against mechanized production methods, the Arts and Crafts architect and designer Charles Voysey (1857–1941) believed that mechanization did have a place in modern furniture design, particularly as the rapid growth of the middle classes created a pressing need for the mass production of furniture. Machines, he argued, would ultimately provide well-designed furniture within the economic reaches of all people and not just the élite, thereby avoiding the paradox of Morris' beautifully handcrafted, 'simple' furniture that was beyond the financial grasp of the masses; even Ashbee came to support Voysey on this point, accusing Morris of 'intellectual Ludditism'.

The interwar years were characterized by the search for new uses of materials and by the desire to use as few components as possible in any one design; minimizing the number of components would not only encourage aesthetic purity but would also, it was hoped, facilitate mechanized production. Ideas from Continental Europe were most influential at this time, with designers such as Gerrit Rietveld, Marcel Breuer and Alvar Aalto experimenting with newly developed materials. New housing built for ordinary working people meant that there was a demand for affordable furniture that would fit into small living spaces, and the modernist ideal of simple, flush surfaces and basic forms with minimal decoration was gradually to enter the public consciousness.

The Dutch furniture designer Gerrit Thomas Rietveld (1888–1964) created some of the most radical designs of this period. He was certainly inspired by the work of Josef Hoffmann, but it was the idea of aesthetics over functionalism that was of greater significance in Rietveld's early furniture. He was profoundly influenced by the artistic work of his

Gerrit Rietveld
Red/Blue chair, 1917–18

Mart Stam
Chair S33, 1926

Marcel Breuer
Cesca chair, 1928

fellow countryman, Piet Mondrian (1872–1944), and the rectilinear designs of Frank Lloyd Wright. Rietveld's early designs are for the most part based on geometric abstracted forms derived from the fine art of the De Stijl movement. Indeed, he became one of the movement's first members when it was founded in 1917 by Theo Van Doesburg (1883–1931) and Mondrian.

De Stijl is regarded by many as the first major 'modern' design movement. The design that exemplifies the movement's style better than any other must be Rietveld's Red/Blue chair of 1917. The chair's form consisted of flat rectilinear pieces of wood, which were painted at a later date in primary colours. This chair was first publicized in an article by Van Doesburg for the 1919 edition of his magazine *De Stijl*, in which he described the Red/Blue chair as 'the abstract-real sculpture of our future interior'.[5] The chair is as much if not more a work of sculpture than a functional piece of furniture. Reyer Kras has described it as 'a three-dimensional realization of the philosophy of the De Stijl movement ... Rietveld redefines the "chair", and does so without precedence'.[6]

A turning point in the history of design that was to alter all existing notions of design education came in 1919, when the architect Walter Gropius merged the two art schools in Weimar, Germany and founded the Staatliches Bauhaus; it was the first time modernist ideas had been promoted in a truly academic context. At the Bauhaus the idea of unity between the arts was stressed and the tutors and their students, or 'masters and apprentices', were urged to be artisans rather than artists. In 1919 Gropius wrote in the institute's prospectus: 'The Bauhaus strives to bring together all creative effort into one whole, to reunify all the disciplines of practical art – sculpture, painting, handicraft, and the crafts – as inseparable components of a new architecture.'[7] There was an interchange of ideas between the De Stijl movement and the Bauhaus: Van Doesburg lectured at the Bauhaus from 1921 to 1922 and in 1923 the Red/Blue chair was included in a general

exhibition at the school, a show which helped to disseminate the modernist Bauhaus design doctrine throughout Europe and America. In 1923, László Moholy-Nagy (1895–1946), the Hungarian Constructivist, became the master of the metalwork studio. Moholy-Nagy encouraged the idea of industrial design and in so doing brushed away the last vestiges of 'craft' at the school. An element of Bauhaus design philosophy, that form must follow the dictates of function and industrial mechanization, was to become a fundamental tenet of the Modern Movement.

Ironically, much of the furniture designed at the Bauhaus was not particularly comfortable or practical – but it was conceived for mass production. The reason for this has much to do with the socialist roots of the school. It was believed by its members that a 'better' society could be achieved through the application of good design; the school attempted to provide functional and aesthetically pleasing design for the masses through the means of large-scale mass production. However, ideology was yet again in advance of technological progress: the furniture was consciously designed to look machine-made, although in reality most of it had to be handcrafted and was therefore costly.

Hungarian-born Marcel Lajos Breuer (1902–81) studied at the Bauhaus, Weimar from 1920 to 1924 and in 1925 became master of the woodwork studios at the Bauhaus in Dessau. He had a profound influence on the evolution of modern design, not only through his later teaching at Harvard but through his furniture designs, which received worldwide recognition and acclaim. In 1925, he designed the Club Chair Model B3, which was to become known as the Wassily chair, named after the artist Wassily Kandinsky (1866–1944), who had asked Breuer to design a chair for his staff house at the new Bauhaus campus in Dessau. The chromium-nickel plated, tubular steel frame with leather or canvas sling back, seat and arms was revolutionary in its application of materials. It is said that the handlebars of his newly purchased

Adler bicycle inspired Breuer's use of a tubular steel construction for this chair. The simplicity, tension of line and spatial qualities of the design are reminiscent of contemporary abstract Constructivist sculpture. Prior to the Wassily chair, metal furniture had been reserved strictly for commercial buildings. The acceptance of this design by Breuer's contemporaries and more importantly by Thonet, the large furniture manufacturer, meant that the Wassily chair changed the public's conception of what a residential interior could include.

An even greater simplicity of form was achieved by Breuer in his cantilevered Cesca chair of 1928, a format that was first applied to furniture by the Dutch architect, Mart Stam (b. 1899), with his Chair S33 of 1926. A year later the German architect and designer, Ludwig Mies van der Rohe (1886–1969), designed his own variations known as the MR chair and the Weissenhof chair. For the first time in the history of furniture, through the cantilever principle and the use of resilient tubular steel, a stable chair could be constructed of only a single-linear frame with two vertical elements. The use of steel tubing allowed these designs to be mass-produced economically using existing industrial technology; this novel method of construction also allowed a minimalism in design and its inherent springiness gave more comfort to the sitter. The manufacture of tubular-steel furniture was banned in Nazi Germany during the 1930s because of its association with the Bauhaus and thereby socialism. Ironically, this type of furniture was favoured by the Fascists in Italy: the architect Giuseppe Terragni was commissioned to design several pieces of tubular metal furniture for the Casa del Fascio in Como. The cantilever chair, however, utilizes more raw materials in its construction than chairs with four legs and its production was therefore limited during the Second World War.

Ludwig Mies van der Rohe was appointed the director of the German government pavilion at the Barcelona International Exhibition of 1929, the year before he was to become director of the Bauhaus (1930–33). The pavilion was furnished with pieces specially designed by him, including two X-framed Model No. MR90 chairs with matching ottomans upholstered in white kidskin. The Barcelona chair, as it was later to become known, exudes a sense of luxury, with its buttoned leather cushions and its ample yet classically inspired proportions and form based on the ancient folding stool known as the *sella curulis*. The chair was specifically designed for use by King Alfonso XIII and his queen at the exhibition's inauguration ceremony. Indeed, this throne-like design can be seen as a precursor to the ultimate executive chair, the 1956 Lounge chair and ottoman designed by Charles Eames (1907–78). Although the Barcelona chair is thoroughly modern in its design its methods of production were not: it was almost entirely handmade, including the welding of the X joint. In its use of costly materials and production methods it could be said to mimic rather than to comply with the Bauhaus socialist design ethic.

The Swiss architect, Charles-Edouard Jeanneret (1887–1965), known as 'Le Corbusier', was a 'modern classicist', like Mies van der Rohe and Walter Gropius with whom he had worked in the Berlin architectural office of Peter Behrens (1869–1940). Le Corbusier initiated a reappraisal of bentwood furniture through his work as an interior designer in the 1920s. He would place Thonet bentwood chairs, designed in the second half of the nineteenth century, in modernist architectural settings, juxtaposing the elegant curves of bent wood with the unrelenting angularity of his residential interiors. The idea of Thonet chairs in anything but a café or a bar would have been unthinkable before this date. One of Le Corbusier's progressive interior schemes was exhibited in the Pavillon de l'Esprit Nouveau at the Paris 'Exposition Internationale des Arts Décoratifs et Industriels Modernes' in 1925, the exhibition from which the term 'Art Deco' was coined. This was the style that superseded Art Nouveau and drew its decorative inspiration from a wide variety of sources, which

Michael Thonet
No. 4 bentwood chair, 1848

Mies van der Rohe
Barcelona chair, 1929

Le Corbusier
Grand Confort, 1928

Eileen Gray
Transatlantique chair, 1926

included ancient Egyptian civilization, tribal art, geometric abstraction, popular culture and the Modern Movement. Unlike their modernist contemporaries, exponents of Art Deco, such as Emile Jacques Ruhlmann (1879–1933), still favoured the idea of handcrafted furniture that relied on costly raw materials such as tropical woods, ivory, silver and even mother-of-pearl. With its inevitable reliance on private patronage and its incompatibility with machine production, even the best of Art Deco was bound to be out-of-step with the ideals of the Modern Movement.

Le Corbusier went on to design a range of tubular steel furniture that was manufactured by Thonet. His Grand Confort armchair was co-designed with his cousin Pierre Jeanneret (1887–1967) and Charlotte Perriand (b. 1903) in 1928 for a villa in Ville d'Avray. The proportions of this armchair and its heavily stuffed upholstery were influenced by Art Deco, yet it achieves a sense of modernity through its use of a tubular steel frame. It was first exhibited, to much acclaim, at the Salon d'Automne, Paris in 1929 together with the Basculant chair and the Model No. B306 chaise longue, also designed in 1928. Charlotte Perriand stated: 'Metal plays the same part in furniture as cement has done in architecture. It is a revolution. If we use metal in conjunction with leather for chairs . . . we get a range of wonderful combinations and new aesthetic effects.'[8] Model No. B306 uses a continuous tubular steel frame with rubber webbing covered in pony skin. The use of contrasting materials, combined with its proportions solely based on the human form and the fact that it could be set in various positions, including rocking, created a harmony between functionalism and aesthetics, making it one of the best-known designs of the twentieth century.

Eileen Gray (1878–1976) was born in Ireland, yet spent most of her life in Paris. She was able to combine the existing Art Deco style prevalent in late 1920s Paris with the new functionalism emanating from Germany to produce a chic style that was very much her own.

The folding Transatlantique chair of 1926 exemplifies this fusing of styles: the angularity of the frame and the slung seat are derived from the Bauhaus, yet the padded leather used for the seat and the use of a lacquered frame are derived from Art Deco. Her designs were expensive to produce and were never intended for large-scale mass production; it was, therefore, inevitable that designs by Gray, like those of Le Corbusier, remained élitist during the 1920s and it was not until the 1970s with the launching of 're-editions' that they became more widely known and influential.

A Finnish proponent of the Modern Movement was the architect and designer, Hugo Henrik Alvar Aalto (1898–1976), who, unlike the majority of his European contemporaries, was more interested in the design potential of plywood than that of tubular metal. His all-wood constructions attempted to prove that a wood laminate was just as valid and modern a material as tubular metal. Aalto strove to design furniture that could be mass-produced; he realized that the fewer components needed, the easier the assembly process. The 41 chair, designed between 1931 and 1932 for the TB sanatorium at Paimio, exemplifies this idea, for the seat and back are constructed from a single piece of bent plywood. Although the technique for bending plywood was invented in the nineteenth century, Aalto made an important improvement to it: where there was a need for greater pliancy, such as in the curve between the back and the seat, he thinned out the veneers by removing several layers, thereby allowing greater malleability. The use of contoured plywood was later to be further advanced by Charles Eames and Paul Goldman (b. 1912) in the 1940s and 1950s respectively. The seat and back section of the 41, or Paimio chair, appear to be suspended between the pair of side frames, an idea Aalto undoubtedly borrowed from Breuer's design for the Wassily chair; it is known that Aalto had ordered a Wassily chair in 1928 for his own use. The Paimio chair is a more minimal and economic design comprising fewer components, only six in total. For some

Gerald Summers
Lounge chair, 1933–34

Bruno Mathsson
Eva chair, 1934

Hans Coray
Landi chairs, 1938

of the other furniture commissioned for the Paimio sanatorium, Aalto did use a combination of bent wood and tubular metal, but he maintained that it was wood that was 'the form-inspiring, deeply human material',[9] thereby promoting a more organic form of modernism. The idea of using less angular forms indicated an important shift in the Modern Movement that was to culminate in the 'free flowing' forms favoured by American and some European designers in the late 1940s and 1950s.

A British designer who was to use bent plywood in a novel way was Gerald Summers (1899–1967). Inspired by the 1933 exhibition of Aalto's work in London, Summers designed his own Lounge chair intended for use in the tropics. Cut and bent from a single length of birch plywood, it pushed the inherent qualities of plywood further than had been achieved previously.

Scandinavian design at this time was particularly notable for its new treatments of wood, which were promoted by the region's abundance of wood as a natural resource. An apparent commitment to functionalism and machine aesthetics emerged from the 1930 Stockholmsustallningen (Stockholm Fair), organized by the architect Gunnar Asplund (1885–1940) – it was Aalto, a Finn, who was the first Scandinavian exponent of this new style – but by the end of the decade the Swedish designer Bruno Mathsson (b. 1907) was again using simple, natural materials to create an impression of luxury. His 1934 Eva chair has a laminated beechwood frame and uses hemp webbing for the seat and back. Mathsson designed the chair to be both aesthetically pleasing and comfortable, declaring, 'the business of sitting never ceases to fascinate me'.[10] Ten years later the Danish designer Hans Wegner (b. 1914) designed the Chinese chair, which again points to the Scandinavian love of simplicity in line and form together with a deep understanding of the intrinsic qualities of natural fibres and woods. Combining natural materials was an essentially Scandinavian approach to furniture design, which continued as the century progressed.

The Butterfly chair, designed in 1938 by the Argentinian architects, Jorge Ferrari-Hardoy, Juan Kurchan and Antonio Bonet, achieves a similar visual simplicity through the use of few components. Occasionally called the Sling chair, it was constructed of a tubular metal frame in sections, making it easy to dismantle and reassemble. It was inspired by a wood and canvas folding Tripolina chair designed by Joseph Beverly Fenby in 1855, which was used by British army officers in the nineteenth century. The Butterfly chair was manufactured under licence by Knoll International but there were also many unlicenced copies made. In the 1950s interest in the Butterfly chair was revived – not surprisingly, as it comprises an abstracted organic form.

In contrast, the highly influential Landi stacking chair designed by the Swiss designer Hans Coray (b. 1906) in 1938 has been called 'proto-High Tech', for like High-Tech furniture designs from the 1970s it makes use of industrial materials, is entirely functional and perfectly suited to mass production. It was commissioned by the architect Hans Fischli for the Landi, the Swiss national exhibition held in Zürich in 1938, where it was received with great acclaim. This innovative design was very progressive in its use of sheets of 'steel hard' tempered aluminium alloy – a sheet was stamped using a drop-press into the required shape and then was punched with large circular holes – which had a distinct crystalline finish. The chair was designed for outdoor use in public parks and was the main source of inspiration for the British designer Rodney Kinsman (b. 1943) when he came to design the Omkstak chair in 1971, which is viewed as a design icon by the functionalist camp of architects and designers.

Completely at odds with the Modern Movement was the development of Surrealism, which made its own bizarre contribution to the classics of twentieth-century furniture design. The Mae West Lips sofa, designed in 1936 by Salvador Dali (1904–89), first appeared in a gouache drawing entitled *Mae West* (1934), depicting an interior

13

in which her lips are represented by a sofa, her nose by a sideboard and her hair by a pair of curtains. The sofa was manufactured around 1936 in Paris for Baron de L'Epée and in London for the great Surrealist art collector, Edward James. The upholstery was covered in a pink satin that was made to correspond with the colour of Schiaparelli's Shocking Pink lipstick. (This sofa was 'redesigned' by Studio 65 using foam upholstery in 1972 and was renamed the Marilyn sofa.) The design readdresses the recurring question of whether furniture can be regarded as art, a matter that was to be widely debated in the early 1980s with 'one-off' anti-functional designs.

The Second World War dramatically affected the development of furniture design in Europe. Earlier, in 1933, Nazi persecution had led to the closure of the Bauhaus and designers such as Moholy-Nagy, Breuer and Mies van der Rohe emigrated to America, designating the United States the new centre of progressive design. Meanwhile, in Europe, it was inevitable that the war would wreak havoc on furniture manufacturing – in occupied France, for example, the industry ceased to exist and would not regain confidence until the mid-1950s.

In Britain during the war, Gordon Russell (1892–1980), who in the 1930s had adopted the principles of modernism, became the Chairman of the Board of Trade and designed a range of 'utility' furniture. Stylistically, these designs owe much to the English Arts and Crafts Movement of the early 1900s, although their methods of production were vastly dissimilar. Throughout the war, furniture – like other goods – was strictly rationed and from 1942 it could only be manufactured under licence from the Board of Trade. These restrictions were not revoked until 1948, although they remained effectively in force until 1952, through a tax on furniture that did not meet the Board's specifications. This meant that the government determined not only the types of furniture produced, but also the manufacturer and the materials used.

In essence the Board of Trade did an admirable job during the war,

providing functional furniture for young couples setting up their first home and families whose houses had been destroyed in the Blitz. However, during the years immediately following the war, commonly known as the period of 'austerity', the British public grew tired of the socialist-inspired utility furniture and no longer wished to have good taste dictated to them by the government.

The only country that had a design industry that was able to remain relatively intact during the war was America. In 1929 the Museum of Modern Art had been founded and from its conception promoted modern, rational design. To the American public, however, the organic modernism of Scandinavian design was more acceptable than the more functional modernist designs that had come out of Germany and France before the war. Furniture designed by Aalto, for example, received an extremely favourable reception when first seen at the 1939 New York World's Fair. This may be because in its use of natural materials and purity of line such furniture is reminiscent of Shaker design and, therefore, had a nostalgic appeal for the American public, similar to that exercised by Arts and Crafts furniture some years before.

This tendency towards organic design became emphatic in the work of the American designer Isamu Noguchi (1904–88), who in 1939 received a commission from A. Conger Goodyear, the President of the Museum of Modern Art, to design a table for his personal use. This table has a highly sculptural articulated base that supports a thick glass top; it is particularly significant as one of the first examples of American organic design and it set a precedent for the use of organic forms as well as organic materials. Asymmetrical and biomorphic furniture design increased in popularity throughout the 1950s, especially in America and eventually led to the organically inspired, surreal Pop furniture of the 1960s.

The newly acquired taste for organic design inspired the 1940 'Organic Design in Home Furnishings' competition at the Museum of Modern

Salvador Dali
Mae West, 1934

Art. Among the judges were Alvar Aalto and Marcel Breuer. Undoubtedly, the most innovative entries were designs submitted by two Cranbrook Academy of Art tutors, Charles Eames and Eero Saarinen (1910–61), working together as a partnership. Of this famous if brief collaboration, Cesar Pelli wrote, 'Eero was worried about form, Eames was worried about how to produce',[11] identifying their ability to create aesthetically pleasing designs that could be mass-produced. Their revolutionary interpretation of organic design was founded on amorphous forms derived from the 'essence' of organic life; they also proposed to manufacture this furniture using state-of-the-art technology. All the chair designs they submitted to the competition employed plywood shells with three-dimensional compound curves; this was the first instance of compound curves – bending wood over two geometric planes – being applied to furniture design. Another remarkable element of the designs they submitted, such as the A3501 series of three chairs, was that Eames and Saarinen had conceived the forms of chairs in accordance with the way people actually sit, rather than according to the way they ought to sit.

This period heralded the beginning of postwar design. In 1941, the 'cycle welding' process was developed by the Chrysler Corporation; it allowed wood to be joined to glass, metal and rubber. In the same year, Charles Eames with his new second wife, Ray (née Kaiser; 1912–89) moved to southern California and set up the Plyformed Products Company. There they developed techniques for producing low-cost wood laminates and mouldings. The Italian-born sculptor, Harry Bertoia (1915–78), who had also studied and taught at Cranbrook Academy of Art, began working with the Eameses in 1943. Their research led the company to be commissioned by the United States Navy to produce leg splints, arm splints and stretchers executed in moulded plywood. Although extremely lightweight the splints were very strong owing to the use of compound curves in their construction. The designers developed new machinery for moulding and bonding plywood which they called the 'KAZAM!' machines, a name derived from the noise they made when operated. Using these new machines they were able to develop various prototype parts for the Vultee BT15 Trainer aeroplane and parts for a working prototype plywood glider known as the CG-16 Flying Flatcar. This in-depth research into moulded plywood and its applications allowed such classic chair designs as the LCW and LCM to be mass-produced after the Second World War.

The developments in modernist ideology between 1900 and 1945 shaped the history of furniture design in this period. It was not until after 1945, however, that modernist ideals could be reconciled with the demands of a mass market. After years of seeing the potential for greater mechanization, but being deprived of the technology that would transform their ideas into reality while maintaining the integrity of their designs, avant-garde designers were at last able to combine the prewar modernist 'vision' with the technology to make it possible, allowing for previously undreamed of possibilities in the furniture manufacturing industry.

Charles Eames
Leg splint, 1942

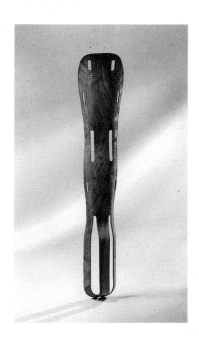

1945 to 1950   Reconstruction and rationalism

16

Finn Juhl
Easy chair, 1945

George Nelson
Platform bench, 1946

Charles Eames
La Chaise, 1948

Carlo Mollino
Armchair for the Minola House,
1944–46

The Second World War dramatically increased the need for better, faster and more cost-effective methods of industrial production. In order to advance manufacturing technology, existing engineering systems had to be upgraded and new materials were developed, for example, synthetic adhesives, lightweight nylon, acrylics, polyesters and polythene resins. After 1945 the American furniture industry, in particular, benefited from this surge of research, as war-related methods of production found useful peacetime applications. Aircraft manufacturing provided the greatest technical resource, with the development of new processes of arc welding, moulding plastics and casting aluminium. A broad range of new materials became available with enormous potential for experimentation: for the first time, standardized mass production of furniture could become a reality.

Like their predecessors – notably Mies van der Rohe, Breuer and Le Corbusier – the architect-designers of the immediate postwar years believed in the machine ethic: that rational use of the machine could directly benefit mankind. 'Mass-productability' was viewed as an integral part of a successful design. The prewar Modern Movement and especially the Bauhaus had concerned itself primarily with production rather than consumption, promoting the ideal of definitive rational designs. Contrary to these socialist precepts, however, the emerging philosophy after the war centred on the realization that consumerism had to dictate production. The postwar International Style was founded in a capitalist and, therefore, consumer-led free market, which demanded continuous development in design. With a new purpose and the flexibility that technology now provided, designers saw their individual works as having quite specific functions and as more subject than ever to the dictates of fashion.

The combined effects of booming consumerism and new technology were most evident in America, which had seen an influx of architects and

designers aligned to the Modern Movement during the 1930s. The Dessau Bauhaus had been dissolved in 1933 and Mies van der Rohe, Marcel Breuer and Walter Gropius, among others, had emigrated to America via Britain, to escape Nazi persecution; as a result, modernism became truly international for the first time. In 1937 Moholy-Nagy established the New Bauhaus in Chicago; this closed in 1938, but he subsequently founded the School of Design, Chicago (1939–44) and in 1944 the Institute of Design, Chicago, both of which upheld modernist principles. Prior to the Second World War, American designers had often looked to the long design history of European decorative arts, but in the mid-1940s a style emerged that was purely American in inspiration, reflecting the public's increased confidence in the United States as a dominant world power. Indeed, by the turn of the decade, European designers were imitating the style championed by the new heroes of American design. The work of Charles Eames and Eero Saarinen had the greatest influence and it consistently appeared in European design journals, such as *Domus* and *Casabella*.

Unlike the devastation in Europe, America's economy, industry and cities were intact after the war, with low unemployment and a new-found prosperity. After the general demobilization, American manufacturers quickly adapted their production to peacetime domestic products, as young couples rushed to get married and set up home. More people than ever before were becoming 'homemakers' and property ownership and the consequent need for domestic furnishings were rapidly increasing. By 1947, the furniture industry had become the second largest producer of retail items in the United States, with designers and manufacturers favouring factory-type mass production that relied on high investment and a fairly static production line. During this period many department stores promoted a modern look for the home as though exorcizing any remaining ghosts of the depression and the war. The slogan, 'Use it up, wear it out,

make it do',[1] which had sustained the American war effort, was no longer applicable.

A wide range of furniture suited to a variety of budgets was available in the United States in the late 1940s, including costly architect-designed furniture and inexpensive facsimiles of it. As domestic interiors became smaller, furniture followed in scale, relating specifically to the needs of the people using it rather than to the architecture surrounding it. Designing furniture with the emphasis on how it was to be used signified an important departure from a former tenet of the Modern Movement; rather than creating furniture within the context of a particular interior, postwar design focused on the action of sitting or on ergonomics.

Increasingly eminent in the postwar years were two American furniture manufacturing giants, Herman Miller Inc. and, slightly later, Knoll International. Both companies were dominated by tutors and graduates from the Cranbrook Academy of Art in Bloomfields, Michigan. The Cranbrook Academy, founded by George G. Booth, a wealthy newspaper baron, can be seen to have been the single most important art and design school in America during the interwar years. The Academy was one of the first European-type design schools to be founded in America and, like the Bauhaus, its aim was to bring art and craft closer together; indeed, Cranbrook has been called 'America's democratic counterpart to the Bauhaus'.[2] During the 1930s the school was directed by the Finnish architect Eliel Saarinen (1873–1950), who encouraged rational design practices. The workshops, or studios, were dedicated to various media – for example, textile design, metalwork, painting and sculpture – and the interchange of ideas between disciplines was actively encouraged. The Academy advocated Eliel Saarinen's philosophy: 'Creative art cannot be taught by others. Each one has to be his own teacher. But connection with the other artists and discussions with them provide sources for inspiration.'[3] Certainly, from its foundation in 1932, the institute attracted the most talented young designers and artists in the United States. It was able to boast of having Charles Eames, Ray Kaiser (Eames), Eero Saarinen, Harry Bertoia, Florence Schust (Knoll, b. 1917), Maija Grotell (1899–1973), Zoltan Sepeshy (1898–1974) and Carl Milles (1875–1955) among its alumni and teaching staff. The concentration of talent had a profound effect on the evolution of the Modern Movement; it was at Cranbrook in the 1930s that organic forms began to appear in furniture design, a development that was to become increasingly significant in international modernism. This creative community – with Herman Miller and Knoll International acting as its commercial catalysts from the 1940s onwards – was to change previously held concepts of furniture design throughout the western world.

The Herman Miller Company, based in Zeeland, Michigan, was established as the small-scale Star Furniture Company in 1905, producing traditional domestic furniture. In 1923, the company became known as Herman Miller, named after the father-in-law and business partner of D.J. De Pree, its chairman and one of its founders. In 1945, the company changed direction and began to compile a collection of elegant furniture that did not follow the dictates of mass public taste and seasonal fashion, but rather set its own trends by promoting aesthetically pleasing, timeless designs. This resulted in a relatively static product line that advanced excellence in design and manufacturing. Dedication to this idea sustained the Herman Miller company through the fickle changes in fashion during the subsequent decades. Many of the 'classic' designs originally produced by the company are just as popular now as when they were first introduced; De Pree described the company's quest for integrity of design when he wrote, 'A design must give the final and inevitable expression of an idea, so that studying it, we say "This is right, this is the way it has to be".'[4]

Another highly influential figure who contributed to the prosperity of the company was George Nelson (1907–86), who trained as an architect at Yale University. In 1945 he was appointed the design director of Herman Miller, replacing the late Gilbert Rohde (1894–1944), whose modernist designs had been difficult to sell in a depressed retail market. De Pree offered him this important position as a direct result of Nelson's design for a wall storage unit, which had been featured in *Architectural Forum* magazine. The built-in compartmental storage unit, which was intended in part as a room divider, was to become a quintessential feature of 1950s interiors. In 1946, Nelson co-wrote with Henry Wright a book entitled *Tomorrow's House*, in which he presented many novel ideas on how living spaces could be most efficiently used. In defence of the storage unit, he wrote, 'Attention to storage units as a factor in providing greater flexibility for living also has a profound effect on the housewife's problems of keeping the place in order.'[5] The advent of built-in storage meant that the emphasis in furniture design was changed forever: fewer pieces of 'case' furniture were necessary, living space was maximized and, as a result, free-standing furniture and in particular the chair was to achieve a greater status.

Compartmentalized storage units were often completely rectilinear and generally utilized a cube-on-cube system. At the same time, chairs and tables were becoming more sculptural in their design and increasingly organic in form. The combination of symmetrical and asymmetrical, architectural and sculptural shapes would create an unusual but harmonic juxtaposition in many interiors during the 1950s. With generally smaller floor areas, the spatial qualities of furniture were emphasized through the use of glass, perspex and aluminium.

In 1946, George Nelson persuaded Charles Eames to design furniture for Herman Miller. Eames had trained as an architect at Washington University, Saint Louis, Missouri and then won a fellowship at Cranbrook Academy, where he later joined the faculty. A year later, Herman Miller began production of the Isamu Noguchi IN50

George Nelson
Basic storage components, 1949

coffee table. Nelson felt sure that these avant-garde designs would appeal to architects and interior designers and specifically targeted his marketing at these design-conscious groups, with great success. The company expanded rapidly and is an American industrial success story: in 1987, Herman Miller Inc. was voted one of 'America's Most Admired Corporations'. This remarkable achievement stems partly from the highly innovative work of Charles and Ray Eames, which brought the company worldwide renown.

Charles and Ray Eames' first project for mass-produced furniture commenced in 1945. They developed a group of children's furniture, comprising a chair, stool and table. Owing to marketing difficulties, only a trial run of 5,000 chairs and stools was produced, by the Moulded Plywood Division of the Evans Products Company. Between 1945 and 1946, however, the Eameses designed a series of highly successful moulded plywood chairs: the LCM (Lounge Chair Metal), the LCW (Lounge Chair Wood), the DCM (Dining Chair Metal) and the DCW (Dining Chair Wood). Available with metal or wooden frames and a variety of finishes, these chairs resulted directly from the Eameses' wartime research into moulding plywood. In 1946, they designed two plywood tables to match the LCW and the LCM, together with a folding plywood screen. In the same year and on the strength of these new designs, the Museum of Modern Art devoted its first one-man show to Charles Eames' innovative work, entitled, 'New Furniture Designed by Charles Eames'. Articulation of the seat and back of each chair was achieved by using a cycle-welding technique, which employed electronically welded rubber shock mounts. This process not only allowed a degree of flexibility, but also enabled wood and metal to be joined together. The use of compound curves in the moulding of the plywood gave the chairs an inherent flexibility and meant that they were comfortable, even though they were not upholstered. The chairs were first manufactured by Evans Products Company – which during the war had taken over the

Eameses' own Plyformed Products Company – and were solely distributed and marketed by Herman Miller. In 1949, there was a period of transition as the manufacturing process itself was taken over by Herman Miller. De Pree was to describe the moulded plywood chair as 'Beautiful, comfortable, easy to move. It's unimprovable. It's a national treasure that ought to be made available'.[6] These highly sculptural chairs, derived from organic forms, were well constructed from the point of view of ergonomics and represent a very successful combination of aesthetics and functionalism.

The Hans G. Knoll Furniture Company was established on the East Coast in the early 1940s, and in 1942 the first Knoll showroom opened in New York. The company was founded by Hans Knoll (1914–55), whose father, Walter, had been an important furniture manufacturer in prewar Weimar Germany, producing designs by Marcel Breuer, Walter Gropius and Mies van der Rohe. Like George Nelson, Hans Knoll quickly realized that architects desired modern furniture designs that would be in keeping with their own innovative buildings. With this in mind he began to work with the Danish designer Jens Risom (b. 1916) during the war, designing simple furniture, using easily available materials such as parachute fabric and army surplus webbing.

Hans Knoll was not drafted into the Forces owing to a history of tuberculosis, so he remained in America operating his furniture company. In 1943 he formed a business partnership with Florence Schust, whom three years later he was to marry. When studying at Cranbrook Academy of Art, Florence Knoll had become friends with Eero Saarinen, Harry Bertoia and Charles and Ray Eames. After completing at Cranbrook she took an architectural degree at the Architectural Association in London, going on to study at the Armour Institute in Chicago under the direction of Mies van der Rohe. In 1946, Hans and Florence formed Knoll Associates Inc., based on Madison Avenue. Soon other European designers, most notably Franco Albini (1905–77) and

Charles Eames
Child's chair, c. 1945

Pierre Jeanneret, were brought in to the Knoll 'fold' on a royalty basis. Florence Knoll concentrated on the design and production side of the business and Hans on the sales and marketing. Both are said to have been perfectionists who focused their attentions on even the smallest of details; this surely was the key to their international success and recognition. The editor of *Architectural Forum*, Howard Meyers, was a close friend of the Knolls and introduced them to Isamu Noguchi, Frank Lloyd Wright and many other influential designers. Meyers was also able to secure their first major interior design contract: for the Rockefeller family's offices in the Rockefeller Plaza, New York. Eventually, interior design was to become as important to the business as retailing. Florence Knoll's interiors were easily recognizable, for her aim was to produce an uncluttered space with clean lines and pure colours, believing that, 'the simpler the background the easier the thought process'.[7] What she achieved was the Knoll 'look', derived primarily from the prewar International Style, but at the same time imbued with colour and eminently suited to the new design of contemporary American homes, offices and showrooms.

Eero Saarinen had first trained as a sculptor in Paris (1930–31) before studying architecture at Yale University. His father, Eliel Saarinen, had been appointed President of Cranbrook Academy in 1932, and in 1936 Eero began teaching at the Academy with Charles Eames, Florence Schust and Harry Bertoia. Two of the most important new designs manufactured from 1945 to 1950 by Knoll Associates were by Eero Saarinen. The Grasshopper chair and matching ottoman, designed in about 1946, were first produced in 1947. The Grasshopper, with its bent plywood construction, looked to prewar Scandinavian modernist design for inspiration; the use of laminated wood was dictated by the postwar shortages of other raw materials. The Womb or No. 70 chair designed by Saarinen in 1946 and first produced by Knoll in 1948 was a great success. Florence Knoll had suggested that he design a chair in which one could curl up. Through its sculptural, organic shape, the chair did allow the sitter to assume a foetal position and hence the name 'Womb' was coined. Using a moulded fibreglass seat shell upholstered in latex foam and supported on tubular metal legs, it was a comfortable and visually attractive design. One of the most important features of the chair was that it enabled the sitter to adopt several casual yet comfortable positions; as Saarinen put it, 'The necessity of changing one's position is an important factor often forgotten in chair design'.[8] In this respect, Saarinen can be seen as the forefather of 1960s designers, such as Pierre Paulin (b. 1927), to whom the sitter's freedom of movement was a central consideration. The Womb chair also fulfils the criteria set by Saarinen's most famous pronouncement: 'A chair is a background for a person sitting in it. Thus, the chair should not only look well as a piece of sculpture in a room when no one is in it, it should also be a flattering background when someone is in it – especially the female occupant.'[9]

In 1948, the Museum of Modern Art staged the 'International Competition for Low-Cost Furniture Design', organized by Edgar Kauffmann Jr and juried by Gordon Russell and Mies van der Rohe, among others. It attracted hundreds of entrants from Europe, Scandinavia and America. What emerged from this competition was furniture design intended for mass production, with simple, uncomplicated shapes, on a scale suited to the smaller postwar living spaces. Rene d'Harcourt outlined the aims of the competition in the introduction to the catalogue: 'To serve the needs of the vast majority of people we must have furniture that is adaptable to small apartments and houses, furniture that is comfortable but not too bulky, and that can be easily moved, stored, and cared for; in other words, mass-produced furniture that is planned and executed to fit the needs of modern living, production and merchandising.'[10] The first prize was awarded to the British designers, Robin Day (b. 1915) and Clive Latimer for a tubular metal and wooden storage unit.

The second prize went to Charles Eames for his armchair, which used a stamped aluminium shell, although when it was later produced for Herman Miller, a single seat shell of thermoset resin reinforced with fibreglass was used instead. This design was easily adaptable for production in different materials and was produced by Zenith Plastics of Gardena, California from 1950 in a number of versions, including the RAR-1 rocking chair. Another experimental design submitted by Eames was a highly sculptural, moulded fibreglass chair named, simply, La Chaise, of which only a full-scale prototype was made.

Unlike their Atlantic counterparts, furniture designers in Britain were still working within the constraints imposed on them through national rationing restrictions. In 1944, the Council of Industrial Design had been set up with the aim of promoting better design in British industry. The Council staged an exhibition in 1946 at the Victoria and Albert Museum in London, entitled, 'Britain Can Make It', which was dubbed by sceptics 'Britain Can't Have It', as many of the products on show were either prototypes or produced solely for export. However, the lack of materials and resources did not deter Ernest Race (1913–64), whose 1945 BA chair was included in the exhibition. In 1946 he founded Race Furniture Limited with engineer J.W. Noel Jordan (1907–74), with the intention of mass-producing modern furniture designs; over 250,000 BA chairs were produced using in total 850 tons of scrap aluminium salvaged from wartime aircraft. This functional dining chair was available with or without arms and had a padded plywood seat upholstered in vinyl, leather or fabric. Like many of Race's designs the BA chair employed up-to-date engineering technology in its manufacture; because it used innovative production methods, the design went on to win a gold medal at the tenth Milan Triennale in 1954. In 1948, Race designed his Wing chair and matching sofa, with buttoned upholstery. These designs were really a modern reworking of two traditional seating formats that, nevertheless,

proved very popular when first introduced.

In Italy, the period immediately following the end of the Second World War became known as the *ricostruzione*. During this time there was a greater emphasis on styling than on technological advances in furniture design. The contrast between American and European manufacturing methods during this period was most pronounced in Italy, where furniture manufacturing was still carried out on a relatively small scale, allowing for adaptability within the marketplace. Italian architect-designed furniture was mainly produced in small workshops with low labour costs. Manufactured in small production runs, this furniture remained exclusive and was generally intended for the export market. 'Design' rather than technology was used to revitalize Italian industry, while 'culture' was employed to rebuild Italy's social framework. From this reliance on design in industry was born the Italian Line, 'compensating brilliantly for technical weaknesses in the product in order to beat the competition'.[11] This style or line was based on simplified and abstracted forms that revealed the function of the design. The forms were not truly dictated by function, however, a fact that illustrates another important difference between American and Italian furniture at this time: in America, furniture was ultimately rational both in terms of function and production, whereas most Italian furniture designers were more concerned with aesthetics and the use of luxury materials.

Financial aid in the form of the Marshall Plan from America promoted the rapid recovery of Italian industry. The coalition government implemented a low-wages policy, allowing manufacturers to create competitively priced products that would be attractive to foreign as well as domestic markets. However, it was not until the late 1950s that Italy enjoyed its economic boom fully, for before 1950 the majority of new furniture was not destined for large-scale production. The important furniture manufacturer

Carlo Mollino
Side chair, *c.*1948

Cassina, for example, produced short runs of designs by Carlo De Carli, Ico Parisi (b. 1916) and Gio Ponti (1891–1979). Small-scale production minimized the manufacturer's risk and enabled him to produce more unusual and progressive designs. This flexibility of production was, in fact, one of the Italian industry's greatest assets, for it allowed manufacturing to evolve in tune with the current fashion.

Pursuing the latest fashion meant also, paradoxically, exploring the potential of traditional materials such as wicker, which were normally associated with craft furniture. In 1950, Franco Albini and Franca Helg designed the Margherita chair, which was constructed from cane. Using this traditional material in a novel way, they were able to produce a thoroughly modern composition, effecting the transformation of a centuries-old, craft-based material into one that could be used in industrial production. Innovative use of forms or materials was extremely important in the revitalization of Italian industry and was a further factor that allowed successful competition with other industrial nations.

Furniture designs from Milan, Turin and Rome at this time were characterized by oozing organic forms, in complete opposition to the rigorous angularity that had come out of the Bauhaus. The Turin-based architect, designer and polymath, Carlo Mollino (1905–73), produced some of the most interesting and innovative designs of the late 1940s, designing highly organic furniture that occasionally touched on the surreal. The forms he created were sleek and streamlined, pointing to his love of car racing, and more specifically speed. Mollino's work was dictated by his belief that everything was 'permissible as long as it is fantastic'.[12] Unlike his contemporaries, Mollino never aligned himself to a large manufacturer, nor was he based in Milan, and for these reasons he has to be considered as outside the mainstream of Italian design. Most of his work was commissioned for specific sites, but other designs were intended for small-scale production in joinery workshops such as Apelli & Varesio, based in

Turin. Mollino had an independent source of wealth and did not have to follow the dictates of a manufacturer, instead producing what he wanted for a small number of wealthy patrons. Although working in relative isolation, his work, sometimes called Turinese Baroque, was highly influential upon designers such as Franco Campo and Carlo Graffi; in other designers' hands the essence of Mollino's designs was often watered down, yet it still formed the basis of what was to become generally known as Italian Styling.

New ideas and concepts in design were quickly promoted throughout Europe and America via journals such as *Domus*, founded by Gio Ponti in 1928 and *Casabella*, edited by Franco Albini between 1945 and 1946. During the period 1945 to 1950 there existed two distinctly different approaches to design: Neo-Rationalism, which promoted simple, functional design, and later Anti-Rationalism, which delighted in styling more sophisticated, exclusive pieces. Albini can be considered the major exponent of Neo-Rationalism whereas Ponti was the champion of Anti-Rationalism. The former advocated a utilitarian stance inspired by architecture, whereas the latter promoted a bourgeois viewpoint that was inspired more by the fine arts and, in particular, sculpture. There was also a political dimension to this difference in attitude, for rationalism was associated with design from the Fascist period – and, ironically, was also advocated by the left-wing Popular Front – so designers attempted to distance themselves from the extremes of Fascism and Communism by turning to Anti-Rationalism, an approach that was increasingly dominant in Italy following the events of 1947.

The first Milan Triennale was organized in 1936; it took over from the five previous Monza Biennale exhibitions, so became known as the sixth Triennale. Following the seventh exhibition in 1940, the Milan shows did not take place during the rest of the war years but were reinstated in 1947, and are still an important stage for designers exhibiting new work. The eighth Milan Triennale of 1947 was held on a much smaller scale than the

Hans Wegner
Chinese chair, 1944

prewar exhibitions. That year's theme was the home, highlighting the demand for postwar housing and attempting to find solutions. Domestic living spaces often had to function as studios or offices as well, so the new furniture had to satisfy these needs simultaneously. The exhibits displayed a distinctly Neo-Rationalist attitude towards furniture design, stressing mass production and the need for low-cost products to fulfil the requirements of the lower social classes, an approach similar to that being followed by many designers in Britain and America. Later in the same year, however, the political party of the Socialists and Communists, the Popular Front, was removed from the coalition government and the Christian Democrats gained sole control. The new political mood was reflected in Italian design; the Anti-Rationalist stance of quality rather than quantity was advocated by furniture designers such as Gio Ponti and was the basis on which Italian furniture and product design in the 1950s began to flourish. Italian designers were more likely than their American and Scandinavian contemporaries to work in several interrelated design disciplines, such as architecture, furniture and product design and interior design. The key to Italian success in the world marketplace was versatility, both in the work of the designers and in the production methods of the manufacturer.

Scandinavian design was to prove equally successful in the 1950s, for it too promoted a gentler, less intimidating form of modernism than that favoured by totalitarian regimes during the war. This approach was already evident during the immediate postwar years, when modernist furniture design in Scandinavia concentrated on the use of natural materials, as exemplified by the work of Danish designer Hans Wegner. Wegner's Peacock chair of 1947 was based on the traditional Windsor chair, with a woven seat and contoured splats related to the human form; its successor, the Classic chair of 1949, showed a similar attention to detail with its traditional cabinet-making

joints, and was destined to be produced only by hand. Wegner seemed determined not to allow quality to be sacrificed to quantity or craft to be surrendered to design. The stressing of truth to materials and craftsmanship over mass production was to remain an important factor in Scandinavian design during the 1950s. Due to its high quality and understated luxury, Scandinavian furniture was highly favoured by architects and interior designers in America.

The years 1945 to 1950 saw exploration into better production techniques and new design solutions, which were to evolve to form the basis of 'Fifties Style'. There emerged three very distinct postwar styles – Italian, American and Scandinavian – all based on the teachings of the Modern Movement. Design was now not only the concern of the architects and designers themselves but of the consumer as well. Retailers promoted furniture by giving it the 'designer label' cachet, indeed, the late 1940s and 1950s saw certain designers such as Charles Eames and Raymond Loewy become household names. This general interest in design helped to strengthen the designer's position in industry. The immediate postwar years made up one of the most important and exciting periods in the history of furniture. At no other time were there so many new materials and methods of production available to designers who now felt a social responsibility to shape the 'brave new world' that was to rise up from the devastation of war.

1 **Eero Saarinen**
Womb chair, 1946

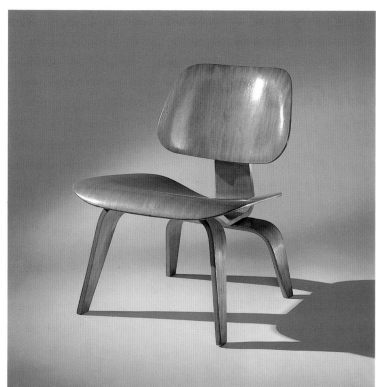

6 **Carlo Mollino**
Writing desk for the Società
Reale Mutua di Assicurazioni,
1948

7 **Carlo Mollino**
Writing desk, 1946

8, 9 **Carlo Mollino**
Roll-top desk for the Mollino
apartment, 1946

10 **Hans Wegner**
Classic chair, 1949

11 (clockwise from left)
Eero Saarinen and Charles Eames
Modular cabinet and bench, 1940

Florence Knoll
Stool, *c.* 1952

Charles Eames
FSW, 1946

Eero Saarinen
Grasshopper chair, *c.* 1946

Harry Bertoia
Diamond chair, 1952

12 **Marco Zanuso**
Antropus chair, 1949

13 **Vladimir Kagan**
Sofa, 1948

Isamu Noguchi
IN50 coffee table, *c.* 1946

14 **Eero Saarinen**
Womb chair with ottoman,
1946

15 **Charles and Ray Eames**
Slunkskin LCW, 1946

16 **Robin Day**
Hillestak chair and desk, 1950

17 **Hans Wegner**
Stacking chairs, 1949

18 **Carlo Mollino**
    Table, *c.* 1949

19 **Carl Jacobs**
    Jason chairs, 1950

20 **Hans Wegner**
   Peacock chair, 1947

21 **Carlo Mollino**
Arabesque tea table, *c.* 1950

22 **Carlo Mollino**
Writing desk for the Orengo
House, 1949

23 **Isamu Noguchi**
Sofa and ottoman, 1946

24 **Isamu Noguchi**
Rudder table, 1949

Notes on the furniture

Dates given are those of *design*, except where stated
Pieces marked with an asterisk* are still in production

Eero Saarinen, American (born in Finland), 1910–61

Womb chair, 1946 (1)
Knoll International, USA

Moulded fibreglass seat shell and loose seat cushions upholstered in fabric-covered latex foam, supported on a chromium-plated or enamelled tubular steel frame, with nylon swivel glides

Eero Saarinen collaborated with Charles Eames on several organic chair designs for the Museum of Modern Art's 'Organic Design in Home Furnishings' competition (1940–41). They won joint first place in two categories with seat furniture that attempted to harmonize form, function and materials. In this search for aesthetically pleasing, unified design, they revolutionized traditional concepts of chair design. Although they managed the consolidation of seat, back and arms in a single moulded plywood shell, Saarinen still considered the legs a problem in visual terms.
The Womb chair, or No. 70, of 1946, first produced by Knoll in 1948, represents Saarinen's pursuance of an organically inspired design in synthetic materials. Like Eames, one of his prime concerns was with human anatomy and its relationship to furniture. The Womb chair perfectly illustrates the intentions of Saarinen and Eames: to create chairs that accommodate people according to the way they actually sit, not the way they ought to sit.
After the No. 70 chair appeared in a Norman Rockwell drawing that was featured in *The New Yorker* magazine, it became known as the Womb chair; its construction was intended to encourage the sitter to curl up into a foetal position and it is considered by many to be one of the most comfortable chairs ever made.

Ernest Race, British, 1913–64

BA chair, 1945 (2)
Race Furniture Ltd, UK

Cast aluminium frame with upholstered, moulded plywood seat and back

The first British mass-produced postwar furniture design, the BA chair's stove-enamelled frame was constructed of resmelted aluminium alloy wartime scrap. Between 1945 and 1964 over 250,000 BA chairs were manufactured from a total of 850 tons of resmelted aluminium. The chair was included in the 1946 'Britain Can Make It' exhibition held at the Victoria and Albert Museum, London. However, it was not until 1951 that it won a Gold Medal at the tenth Milan Triennale for its innovative use of materials.

Charles Eames, American, 1907–78

Birch LCW, 1946 (3)
Herman Miller Inc., USA

Birch-veneered moulded plywood seat and back, attached with rubber shock mounts to a frame of bent birch plywood

Out of earlier experimentation, which was carried out in collaboration with Eero Saarinen and Ray Eames, Charles Eames produced the LCW (Lounge Chair Wood). After exhibiting the chair at the Museum of Modern Art in New York, the California-based firm Evans Products Company manufactured it from 1946 to 1949, after which time Herman Miller took over the chair's manufacture from 1949 to 1957. A dining version was also produced (DCW), as were two versions with metal legs (LCM and DCM). A variety of finishes was available, which included leather, 'slunkskin' (*see* colour plate 15) or fabric upholstery and wood veneers, as well as aniline-dyed variations in black, red or yellow. The LCW and the other chairs of the Moulded Plywood series were highly suited to mass production: they were manufactured in component form with the fewest possible parts using a minimum of materials.

Charles Eames, American, 1907–78

DCM, 1946* (4)
Herman Miller Inc., USA

Walnut-veneered, moulded plywood seat and back, attached with rubber shock mounts to tubular steel legs with self-levelling feet

The DCM (Dining Chair Metal) forms part of Charles Eames' series of Moulded Plywood chairs, which were originally available in a variety of finishes – including mahogany, rosewood, ash, zebrawood and teak veneers as well as leather, 'slunkskin' (*see* colour plate 15) and fabric upholstery – and were also available in two heights, dining and lounging. The walnut versions were manufactured from 1946 to 1957, and were reissued in 1962. A matching low table with metal legs was also designed in 1946. The series was manufactured by Evans Products Company between 1946 and 1949 and was marketed and distributed exclusively by Herman Miller, who later in 1949 took over the production of the chairs.

4

Ernest Race, British, 1913–64

BA armchair, 1945 (5)
Race Furniture Ltd, UK

5

Cast-aluminium frame with upholstered moulded plywood seat and back

Like the side chair version, the BA armchair was manufactured by Ernest Race's own company. Race and his partner Noel Jordan established Ernest Race Ltd (later to become Race Furniture Ltd) in 1945. The company aimed to provide well-designed, high-quality yet affordable furniture for the British public.

Carlo Mollino, Italian, 1905–73

Writing desk for the Società Reale Mutua di Assicurazioni, 1948 (6)
Probably Ettore Canali, Italy

Solid oak construction with Fibrosil laminated top

6

In 1946, Carlo Mollino was commissioned to design a wide variety of desks, tables and chairs for the offices of the Reale, Turin. This desk and other variations from the Reale series were inspired by aeronautical engineering. Utilizing solid wood trestles, diagonal braces, stringers and Y-shaped supports, these desks appear more rationally conceived than Mollino's more fluid furniture pieces, such as the Arabesque table or the Singer table (*see* colour plates 21 and 22). The desk illustrated is able to rotate around the drawer unit, providing a high degree of flexibility for the user. When this series was designed the synthetic laminates used on some of the desk tops, such as Fibrosil, were still in their infancy and were considered luxury materials.

Carlo Mollino, Italian, 1905–73

Writing desk, 1946 (7)
Probably Ettore Canali, Italy

Solid oak construction

This boldly constructed desk from the Reale series has a detachable drawer unit. The series was highly influential and continues to inspire contemporary designs, such as the Briol chairs designed by Konstantin Grcic in 1990 (*see* colour plate 144).

7

Carlo Mollino, Italian, 1905–73

Roll-top desk for the Mollino apartment, 1946 (8, 9)
Apelli & Varesio, Italy

Stained maple frame supporting maple roll top fitted with brass screws

8

9

This highly unusual desk was designed by Mollino for his own use in his bachelor studio flat in Turin. The desk was conceived so that when the roll top was in the down position, the sides could be dropped, allowing it to be used as a table. The prototype for the desk was of larger proportions, but owing to technical difficulties the size was subsequently reduced in the final design. The small Turin-based workshop of Apelli & Varesio constructed this elegant piece of furniture, which is now in the Christina and Bruno Bischofberger Collection, Zurich.

Hans Wegner, Danish, b. 1914

Classic chair, 1949* (10)
Johannes Hansen Mobelsnedkeri, Denmark

10

Solid teak construction with woven cane seat

Originally named the Round chair because of its shape, it soon became referred to as the Classic or sometimes The Chair. Designed early in Wegner's career, the Classic chair illustrates that craftsmanship and modern design can operate in harmony. It was constructed almost entirely by hand and ran counter the modernist tenets of mass production. As is the case with many of Wegner's designs the proportions of the Classic chair derive from careful

anatomical study of the human form. Most of his handcrafted furniture was produced by Johannes Hansen in Denmark, while the production pieces were manufactured by another Danish company, Fritz Hansen.

Designs by Cranbrook Academy of Arts alumni (11)

(11, *left*)
Eero Saarinen, American (born in Finland), 1910–61 and **Charles Eames**, American, 1907–78

Modular cabinet and bench, 1940
Eero Saarinen/Charles Eames

Solid wood construction

11

The cabinet and bench were designed by Eero Saarinen and Charles Eames specifically for the Museum of Modern Art's competition, 'Organic Design in Home Furnishings', which was organized in 1940 by Eliot Noyes (1910–77), the first director of the museum's Industrial Design Department. The Eames and Saarinen collaboration produced some of the most innovative and influential designs of the postwar period. A storage-unit format similar to that developed by Eames and Saarinen was adopted by George Nelson in 1947: his Basic Cabinet series also included platform benches with matching cabinets.

(11, *left*)
Florence Knoll, American, b. 1917

Stool, *c*. 1952
Knoll International, USA

Laminated wood seat supported on painted metal rod base

Florence Knoll's furniture designs, like the stool illustrated, have a rational simplicity and a modest, unassuming appearance.

(11, *top right*)
Charles Eames, American, 1907–78

FSW, 1946
Herman Miller Inc., USA

Moulded plywood elements connected with canvas strips

The FSW (Folding Screen Wood), developed from earlier wartime experiments with moulded plywood, was constructed from a series of 9½ inch-wide (24 centimetres wide) U-shaped elements, which were joined to each other with canvas strips. Originally, Eames had attempted to connect the eight plywood sections with flexible vinylite tape. The screen was available in either birch or ash and in two heights, either 34 inches or 68 inches (86.4 or 172.7 centimetres) and could be arranged in various free-standing positions, without the need of supports. The undulating form of the the screen makes its construction appear more complicated than it actually is. Not only is it very compact when folded, it is also extremely light and could be easily transported. In 1955, Herman Miller discontinued production of the screen owing to the increasing costs associated with the insertion of the canvas hinge.

(11, *right*)
Eero Saarinen, American (born in Finland), 1910–61

Grasshopper chair, *c.* 1946
Knoll International, USA

Bent plywood frame supporting upholstered plywood seat with fabric covering

The Grasshopper or No. 61 lounge chair was Saarinen's first furniture design for Knoll International and was available with a matching ottoman. Its simple, economic form is reminiscent of prewar Scandinavian design. The choice of laminated wood for its construction was mainly the result of the postwar limitations on other suitable materials. The chair and ottoman were in production from 1947 to 1965. Florence Knoll said of the Grasshopper: 'It was a perfectly nice chair but it wasn't one of the great successes' (*see* E. Larrabee and M. Vignelli, *Knoll Design*, 1981).

(11, *foreground*)
Harry Bertoia, American (born in Italy), 1915–78

Diamond chair, 1952*
Knoll International, USA

Hand-bent and welded steel rod construction, either chromium-plated or with a white nylon finish

Although Bertoia considered himself foremost a sculptor rather than a furniture designer, he was encouraged by Hans and Florence Knoll to produce a series of bent steel rod chairs utilizing technology developed as a result of the war effort. The Diamond chair was designed for interior

and exterior use and there were several options available, including one that was fully upholstered and another that was especially wide. This unusual yet extremely elegant seating solution was – in its application of materials, at least – unlike any other metal seat furniture of its day. The fact that the Diamond chair is still in production is a fitting tribute to its enduring functionalism and aesthetic.

The black ceramic vase was designed by Maija Grotell in about 1948 and the beige ceramic bottle with stopper was designed by Laza McVey in the late 1940s. The fabric draped over the Diamond chair was designed by Ray Eames around 1955.

Marco Zanuso, Italian, b. 1916

Antropus chair, 1949*(12)
Arflex, Italy

Moulded plywood upholstered in foam rubber, covered in woven fabric

Marco Zanuso was commissioned by the Pirelli Company in 1948 to investigate the potential of foam rubber as a material suitable for upholstery. The Antropus chair is an early design, incorporating this novel form of upholstery which did not require traditional springing; the form of the chair was made possible only through the use of this new material. Arflex (established in March 1950), a division of the Pirelli Company, produced Marco Zanuso's innovative furniture. Still in production, the Antropus chair possesses a sophisticated, undulating line that is characteristic of many postwar Italian furniture designs.

Vladimir Kagan, American (born in Germany), b. 1928

Sofa, 1948 (13)
Kagan Designs, USA

Fabric-covered upholstery on a solid wood frame

This 1948 sofa is typical of work from the late 1940s and 1950s by New York designer Vladimir Kagan. The sofa's bold, curving lines exemplify Kagan's confident use of biomorphic forms during these years. The tweed-like textile used for the upholstery was designed by Henry Dreyfuss, Kagan's partner, while the base was carved from solid walnut. The high-quality materials and labour-intensive techniques involved meant that, like much of Kagan's work, this piece was fairly expensive.

13

Isamu Noguchi, American, 1904–88

IN50 coffee table, *c.* 1946* (13)
Herman Miller Inc., USA

Articulated solid walnut base supporting a plate glass top

In 1939, as a result of a commission from A. Conger Goodyear, the president of the Museum of Modern Art, Noguchi designed the Goodyear table, which was made up of an articulated base sculpted in solid rosewood which supported a thick plate glass top. The Goodyear represents one of the first examples of organic design and set a precedent in America for biomorphic forms in furniture. The IN50, or Noguchi, coffee table was a smaller, simplified version of the Goodyear and was produced by Herman Miller between 1947 and 1973. The bases have also been offered in cherry, birch, ebonized poplar and ebonized walnut. The IN50 was reissued briefly in 1980 and again in 1984.

Eero Saarinen, American (born in Finland), 1910–61

Womb chair with ottoman, 1946 (14)
Knoll International, USA

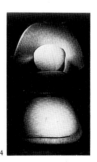

14

Moulded fibreglass seat shell and loose seat cushions upholstered in fabric-covered latex foam, supported on a chromium-plated or enamelled tubular steel frame with nylon swivel glides

The Womb or No. 70 chair designed by Saarinen in 1946 and manufactured by Knoll from 1948 was a great success. Following Florence Knoll's suggestion that he design a chair in which one could curl

up, Saarinen created a sculptural and organically inspired seat shell that was constructed of moulded fibreglass. The ottoman, or No. 74, increased the sitter's freedom to adopt a variety of comfortable positions.

Charles Eames, American, 1907–78 and **Ray Eames,** American, 1912–89

Slunkskin LCW, 1946 (15)
Herman Miller Inc., USA

Slunkskin-upholstered, moulded plywood seat and back, attached with rubber shock mounts to a frame of bent walnut plywood

15

This version of the LCW (Lounge Chair Wood) upholstered in 'slunkskin' (animal hide) was manufactured from 1948 to 1953. It is surprisingly comfortable to sit on, for the rubber shock mounts give the back an inherent flexibility. The electronic cycle-welding process initially used to fuse these connecting mounts to the seats, backs and frames of the moulded plywood chairs was first developed in the 1930s by the Chrysler Corporation. However, after only partial success with this technique, the mounts were glued to the chairs with a resorcinol phenolic adhesive that was applied with heat and pressure.

Robin Day, British, b. 1915

Hillestak chair and desk, 1950 (16)
Hille International & Co. Ltd, UK

Solid beech frame constructions supporting laminated, American walnut chair seat, back and desk top

16

Unlike Eames, Robin Day did not have the technology available to produce furniture with compound curves economically.

45

Undeterred, Day went on to design the Hillestak chair, which used in its construction plywood that had been moulded in a single direction. Designed the same year in which Day was appointed design director at Hille, the Hillestak attempted to bring to the British public good-quality, yet low-cost, contemporary furniture. The matching desk with its trestle-like construction had a removable drawer unit so that it could be easily transformed into a table.

Hans Wegner, Danish, b. 1914

Stacking chairs, 1949 (17)
Fritz Hansen, Denmark

Solid teak or beech frame with plywood seat

17

Although partly machine-made, the Stacking chair appears beautifully handcrafted and possesses an honest simplicity that is reminiscent of Shaker furniture. The three-legged stacking chair was constructed solely from wood using traditional joining techniques.

Carlo Mollino, Italian, 1905–73

Table, *c.* 1949 (18)
Apelli & Varesio, Italy

Solid maple frame construction supporting a plate-glass top and lower plate-glass tier with brass mounts

18

Mollino originally designed the prototype of this table for the Singer Store, Turin. The free-form top and 'floating', leaf-shaped lower tier are attached to the honey-coloured frame with brass mounts that appear to pierce the glass. The refined delicacy of the construction gives this table an appearance of lightness, while the sleek, streamlined form points to Mollino's love of speed (he was a racing car enthusiast and an accomplished automotive designer – his

aerodynamically profiled Osca 1100 won its class at the 1954 Le Mans race). Mollino's furniture was manufactured in four workshops based in Brescia and Turin: Apelli & Varesio, Tesio & Ferrero, Rossi & Celerino, and Ettore Canali. The Singer table is known through photographic documentation to have been produced in the Apelli & Varesio workshop.

Carl Jacobs, Danish, b. 1925

Jason chairs, 1950
Kandya Ltd, UK

19

Solid beech frame supporting bent beech-veneered plywood seat
Carl Jacobs worked between 1950 and 1951 as a designer for Kandya Ltd, a company based in Middlesex, England. During this short period he designed his best-known piece of furniture, the Jason chair, which was inexpensive to produce and was marketed as a stacking contract chair. The seat and back section was formed from a single piece of plywood, which was bent without the use of steaming. The sheet of beech-veneered plywood was cut with a spindle-router and was bent into shape with a pneumatic jig. The interlocking section was then secured in place with a synthetic resin glue applied by hand. The chair took a considerable amount of time to develop: twenty-seven prototypes were made before the design was finally perfected. The seat section of the chair was extremely strong, so much so that Kandya Ltd would demonstrate the chair's resilience by having a person sit on it, while another person balanced on top of the chair's back.

Hans Wegner, Danish, b. 1914

Peacock chair, 1947*(20)
Johannes Hansen Mobelsnedkeri, Denmark

Solid ash and teak construction

The Peacock chair was inspired by the hoop-form of the traditional Windsor chair. Wegner, however, enlarged the proportions with the use of the radiating splat construction from which the chair's name derives; the configuration is reminiscent of a fanned peacock's tail. These spindle-like elements were arranged

20

in such a way as to afford the sitter the greatest amount of comfort.

Carlo Mollino, Italian, 1905–73

Arabesque tea table, *c*. 1950 (21)
Apelli & Varesio, Italy

Pierced and moulded plywood frame supporting plate-glass top and lower tier with brass fittings

Carlo Mollino's most fluid and organic design, as well as his most popular and sought-after, is the Arabesque table. There are several versions in existence. Like those of the Singer table, the glass top and lower tier, which are securely attached to the frame with brass elements, appear to be suspended in air. At a time when Charles Eames and Eero Saarinen were exploring the functional possibilities of moulded plywood, Mollino was exploiting its expressive potential to the full. He was perhaps thinking of the dramatic and flamboyant forms of these designs when he stated that, 'The best explanation of one's work is contained in its silent ostentation' (*see Carlo Mollino Cronaca*, exhibition catalogue, Galeria Fulvio Ferrari, Turin 1985, page 15).

21

22

Carlo Mollino, Italian, 1905–73

Writing desk for the Orengo House, 1949
Apelli & Varesio, Italy (22)

Security plate-glass top supported by brass-mounted marbrite drawer unit and parallel maple legs with single marbrite drawer

The commission for the Orengo House was Mollino's last major interior design project and this unique writing desk was designed site specific for it. Its pierced form was influenced by earlier furniture designed by Antoni y Cornet Gaudí. Also inspired by the interiors of the 1930s, Mollino combined the rich colour of the maple legs with the black marbrite draw units.

Isamu Noguchi, American, 1904–88

Sofa and ottoman, 1946 (23)
Herman Miller Inc., USA

Tapering solid birch legs supporting fabric-covered, upholstered seat and back

Noguchi's sofa IN70 and ottoman IN71 were considered too avant-garde for full-scale mass production but were manufactured by Herman Miller for a brief period (1949–51). These highly sculptural designs were fully upholstered and employed elegant biomorphic forms. Although the sofa was rather large, it achieved a sense of lightness through the subtle tapering of the wooden legs.

23

24

Isamu Noguchi, American, 1904–88

47

Rudder table, 1949 (24)
Herman Miller Inc., USA

Solid birch top supported on two parabolic, bent metal legs and one solid birch leg

This 1949 design is often referred to as the Rudder or Parabolic table owing to the shape of its legs and top. Noguchi designed this table in two alternative heights, coffee (IN52) and dining (IN20), and with two finishes, birch and ebonized. The dining table also had matching stools (IN22). All were produced by Herman Miller between 1949 and 1951. As Noguchi explained: 'If my tables suggest landscape, you must be aware that every garden is a landscape, and every garden can be considered a table, too, especially Zen gardens' (*see Isamu Noguchi: Space of Akari and Stone*, exhibition catalogue, Siebu Museum of Art, 1985, page 13).

1950 to 1960   The ascendancy of organic design

Robin Day
Butterfly cocktail cabinet, 1951

William Katavolos, Ross Littell
and **Douglas Kelley**
3LC or T chair, 1952

Franco Albini
PS16 rocking chair, 1956

2

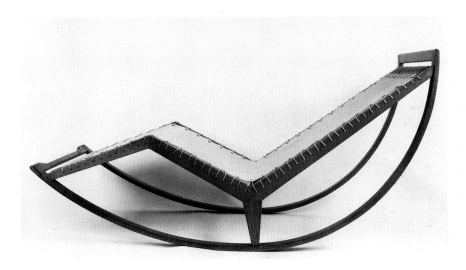

By the year 1950, America
and Western Europe were clearly
recovering from the effects of the
Second World War. A remarkable
economic boom followed industrial
regeneration and with the new-found
prosperity a spirit of idealism swept
over society. As the actress Audrey
Hepburn recalled: 'I remember the
Fifties as a time of renewal and of
regained security. There was a rebirth
of opportunity, vitality and enthusiasm
.... Once again one was allowed to be
optimistic about the future.'[1]

Advances in international
communications fostered a climate of
unprecedented cultural exchange, but it
was cinema, more than any other
medium, that expressed the affluence of
the period through Hollywood's
portrayal of the American dream.
What became abundantly clear was
that economic prosperity and a
desirable way of life were dependent on
the relationship between efficient
industrial systems and mass
consumerism. Better product and
industrial design led to the
development of domestic labour-saving
devices that allowed more time to be
allocated to the pursuit of leisure
activities. In the United States, new
products were designed to look 'modern'
and were targeted at a younger
consumer market which viewed the
future with growing confidence.

Painting and sculpture thrived
during the 1950s, due mainly to the
vitality of a new American movement
in fine art, Abstract Expressionism.
Prior to the Second World War,
Constantin Brancusi (1876–1957) was
one of the first artists to work in an
abstracted form of sculpture that
derived its inspiration from the natural
world. Two of his students, Henry
Moore (1898–1986) and Isamu
Noguchi, continued developing an
abstract organic style after the war,
with Moore concentrating on the
human figure and Noguchi on natural
landscapes. The idea common to such
artists, of paring down form derived
from nature until left with an abstract
essence of the subject, had a strong
influence on designers throughout the
decade and led to a proliferation of
free-form, asymmetrical furniture.

Ernest Race
Advertisement for BA chairs in *Shipbuilding and Shipping Record*, May 1957

Ernest Race
Antelope chair and table, 1951

The ascendancy of organic design in the 1950s did represent a conscious movement away from the geometric formalism of the Modern Movement, but most of the freer, more expressive forms that resulted were still subject to highly technical, mechanized mass production in order to meet the demands of a growing consumer market. After 1950, design was to become more aligned to the sciences than ever before, through engineering, organic chemistry and ergonomics. The furniture industry realized how essential rational design practices were to its success in the marketplace and required designers to have a firm understanding of new production methods and their applications. While the principles underpinning British, American, Italian and Scandinavian design were interrelated, however, the end products retained distinct national characteristics. These variations in style were to become pronounced throughout the 1950s, despite the common belief among the majority of designers that 'good design' now derived from technology rather than craft.

In 1951, the Festival of Britain was staged throughout the United Kingdom as a year-long celebration of British achievement in the arts, sciences, architecture and industrial design. The focus of the exhibition was the newly built Royal Festival Hall and the nationwide festival included ten thousand products overseen by the Council of Industrial Design. Ernest Race designed the innovative Antelope chair, among other pieces of furniture, for the outside terraces at the South Bank exhibition. Working within the constraints of national rationing, Race produced a functional and aesthetically pleasing chair which utilized an efficient metal rod and bent plywood seat construction. The chair's spindly leg, terminating in a spherical foot, became a very common motif in the 1950s. The ball and stick arrangement, similar in appearance to molecular models, reflected an increasing interest in nuclear physics.

Race Furniture Ltd was not the only pioneering company in British furniture design. Hille, a long-established manufacturer, commissioned its first modern designs in 1949 from Robin Day, who had come to the company's attention when he won first prize at the Museum of Modern Art's 'International Competition for Low-Cost Furniture Design'. In 1950, Day became Hille's design consultant and during the same year designed the Hillestak chair and desk which, like Charles Eames' bent ply seat furniture, were intended for low-cost and large-scale mass production. A year later, Day designed the auditorium for the Royal Festival Hall and his upholstered, moulded plywood chairs were used in the indoor public spaces for the duration of the Festival. The Festival heightened the public's awareness of the need for modern design and industry was able to respond to public enthusiasm more fully in 1952, when the tax on non-utility furniture was lifted.

One designer whose innovative designs were produced in large numbers in America was Harry Bertoia. Having worked with Charles and Ray Eames during the war, in the late 1940s Bertoia worked alongside Eames at Evans Products on the project that encompassed the development of the bent ply chairs. As he was a sculptor as well as a designer, it is not surprising that Bertoia approached furniture design from a highly aesthetic viewpoint; this is illustrated by his Diamond chair of 1952, one of the most influential designs to come out of the United States in this period. Like Race's Antelope chair of the previous year, the Diamond chair based its construction on metal rod. Rather than following a traditional chair format, however, Bertoia bent and welded an open steel latticework into a flowing, sculptural configuration which elegantly balanced aesthetics and functionalism. As Bertoia explained: 'When you get right down to it, the chairs are studies in space, form and metal too. If you will look at them, you will find they are mostly made of air, just like sculpture. Space passes right through them.'[2] Bertoia was constantly searching for perfection in design: 'The urge for good design is the same as the urge to go on living. The assumption is that somewhere hidden, is a better way of doing things.'[3]

While many American designers embraced organic design, some, such as William Katavolos (b. 1924), Ross Littell (b. 1924) and Douglas Kelley (b. 1928), preferred to work within an extension of Modern Movement functionalism. Between 1949 and 1955 they established a partnership advocating a stringently rational philosophy, aiming 'to work through to a way of beauty usefully conceived in essential structure, intrinsically materialized and appropriately performed'.[4] Architecturally influenced, their New Furniture Group of 1952 consisted of chairs and tables in leather, chrome-plated steel and glass. The year 1952 also saw the production of their 3LC chair, later labelled the 'T' chair. This three-legged dining chair was constructed from four T-shaped elements and a sling seat; a remarkable innovation of the design was the method with which the leather sling was secured to the legs. Utilizing concealed screws, this construction detail predates Charles Eames' use of a similar system in his Aluminium Group by six years. The 3LC won the A.I.D. (American Industrial Design) award for furniture design in 1952 and was included in the Good Design exhibitions in both 1953 and 1955. Intended as vehicle to promote rational design, these exhibitions were organized by the Museum of Modern Art and held biannually in New York and Chicago from 1950 until 1955.

Throughout the 1950s, Charles and Ray Eames continued to design furniture for Herman Miller, as Peter Smithson described: 'In the 1950s the whole design climate was permanently changed by the work of Charles and Ray Eames .... They use aluminium castings and wire-struts which remind one (but only if one thinks about it) of old and new aeroplanes, not of other furniture .... They have high object-integrity.'[5] The Eameses' first success of this decade was a series of Wire Mesh chairs developed between 1951 and 1953. These chairs, like Bertoia's Diamond chair, used latticed steel rods in the construction of a continuous seat and back. They were marketed as

multi-functional, suitable for 'writing, dining or lounging' and met the demands of the suburban homeowners' market, which required dual-purpose furniture.

In 1956, Charles and Ray Eames created their best-known design, the Lounge chair 670 with matching ottoman 671. Following the traditional English, buttoned-leather club chair, the Lounge chair 670 is unashamedly masculine. It exudes a sense of executive power and wealth through its generous proportions and use of rosewood veneer, sumptuous down-filled upholstery and buttoned-leather covering. The Lounge chair is an eloquent status symbol which confidently demonstrates that modern mass-produced furniture can be both comfortable and luxurious.

Like the Eames office, George Nelson Associates employed a team of in-house designers, and made several important contributions to furniture design during the 1950s. All projects were overseen by George Nelson and are therefore usually attributed to him. The Coconut chair of 1956, designed by George Mulhauser, consisted of a foam-upholstered steel shell supported by three thin, chrome-plated steel legs and was available with a matching elliptical ottoman. The chair is visually light in weight – the wedge-like seat shell appears to hover in space – but is, in fact, surprisingly heavy and derives its name from a cracked section of coconut which inspired its form.

During the 1950s Nelson Associates still faced competition from Knoll International, although Knoll was concentrating increasingly on corporate clients. Eero Saarinen, who continued to design for Knoll, spent much of the decade working on architectural projects such as the Trans World Airlines terminal at John F. Kennedy Airport, New York (1956–62). Saarinen advocated an organic and fluid approach to architecture and design, in opposition to the angularity of Modern Movement rationalism. Between 1956 and 1957 he designed the revolutionary Pedestal Group. Saarinen intended the chairs' construction to be achieved through a single moulding process, but

51

George Nelson
Coconut chair, 1956

unfortunately the technology available in the plastics industry was not sufficiently advanced at this point; as a compromise, a plastic-coated aluminium base was used to support the fibreglass seat shell, effecting the appearance of a single and unified structure. Saarinen's use of the pedestal base was the first of its kind in furniture design. Accomplishing a purity of form, the concept behind Saarinen's elegant Tulip Collection was to clean up the 'slum of legs'.[6]

Two other designers who broke through technological barriers in designing plastic furniture were Erwine and Estelle Laverne (b. 1909 and 1915), who in 1957 launched the Invisible group of chairs, comprising the Lily, Buttercup, Daffodil and Jonquil, which, as their names suggest, possessed forms derived from simple organic shapes. These chairs were constructed of moulded transparent perspex (plexiglass), so provided a remarkable sense of space and light when placed in an interior.

New plastics technology was developed alongside continuing refinements of the processes of bending and moulding plywood. During the Second World War, Paul Goldman, like Charles Eames, supplied the United States military with bentwood products made by his Massachusetts-based company, Plycraft Incorporated. After the war, Goldman continued manufacturing furniture and in 1957 he designed the extremely graceful Twisted armchair with matching side chair. Based on the earlier Nelson Associates Pretzel chair by John Pile, which Goldman helped develop, the Twisted armchair was constructed of walnut- or birch-veneered laminated wood, bent into a series of compound curves. As a marketing strategy, the chair's design was attributed to Norman Cherner, a well-known American furniture designer of the period. It was known as the Cherner chair and both upholstered and non-upholstered variations were manufactured by Plycraft until about 1970. A later, heavier and stronger version, designed by Goldman, replaced the Cherner chair and became known as the Rockwell, following its

appearance in a drawing by the artist Norman Rockwell.

Vladimir Kagan, unlike the majority of his contemporaries in America, favoured a more exclusive approach to furniture design, similar to that of Italian designers Ico Parisi and Carlo De Carli. Using solid wood, usually walnut, Kagan created supremely elegant, streamlined furniture, often upholstered in tweed-like textiles designed by his partner, Henry Dreyfuss. Kagan's furniture was made largely to commission and was relatively expensive, owing to its labour-intensive construction and use of high-quality materials.

Italian furniture design flourished between 1950 and 1960. Because of a shortage of architectural briefs during this period, many highly trained architects turned their talents to designing furniture and consumer products. This surge of creative activity helped Italy to achieve international recognition and unprecedented economic and industrial growth. By 1951, the Milan Triennale had returned to its prewar scale and had re-established its significance in the international exchange of ideas, an exchange further promoted through publications such as *Domus*.

Although most Italian architect-designers had been trained in a rationalist tradition, during the early part of the decade very little furniture was designed for mass production; the capital funding and technology required for large-scale manufacturing was not yet available in Italy. By the mid-1950s, however, the wealthier society that had evolved adopted an American pattern of consumerism. To meet this growing demand for consumer goods, the technology for mass production was developed and applied to furniture for the first time. Rather than commit themselves to static product lines and high investment, manufacturers achieved a continuous output of innovative design through the flexibility of shorter production runs. Though never able to compete in scale with the product-design industry, Italian furniture manufacturers contributed to the 'economic miracle'.

Piero Fornasetti
Mosaic table, *c.* 1955

Contemporary design was well received in Italy in the 1950s, because of its earlier association with luxury and exclusivity. In the late 1940s and early 1950s the exaggerated and sculptural forms of the Milan School, in particular, were seen to express Italy's new wealth, enthusiasm and confident spirit. This highly styled Italian Line was replaced in the late 1950s by the sleek rationalism of the Postwar International Style. Simple, refined designs with spare profiles were practical in terms of production: the fewer components, the easier the assemblage and the lower the cost of materials. Gio Ponti's Superleggera 699 chair, a sophisticated and elegant reinterpretation of a traditional fisherman's chair from Chiavari, near Genoa, was light yet extremely strong in construction. The Superleggera was also very reasonably priced and fulfilled the criteria required for successful mass production. It was first manufactured in 1957 by Cassina and its subsequent retail success led Ponti to design other types of furniture, as he put it, 'without adjectives': classic design that could not be labelled anti-rational, rational, organic and so on.

In the late 1930s, Gio Ponti had met and later formed a collaboration with Piero Fornasetti (1913–88), who was one of the great anomalies of Italian postwar furniture design. Fornasetti was totally opposed to the acknowledged canons of 1950s design and declared: 'I married decoration to form at a time when decoration was being rejected and banished';[7] his use of decoration for its own sake was far removed from the philosophy of modernism. Unlike the majority of his contemporaries, who came from an architectural background, Fornasetti had trained in fine art. He used classical motifs and superimposed them on modern, streamlined forms, juxtapositions that were central to his work and were intended as a jibe at the elevation of pretentious academic art.

Fornasetti was extraordinarily prolific, producing over 11,000 designs for furniture, ceramics, glass and other objects during his lifetime. This abundance of creativity was admired by Ponti: 'He possesses something of that ancient wisdom of past Italian masters; with their imaginative thinking, their playful fancy, their knowledge of all the materials used in their art, their patience and slowness.'[8] The Ponti-Fornasetti partnership created some of the most interesting limited-production furniture of this period and in some ways the collaboration was a happy marriage of contradictions. Ponti's designs were always restrained, pure and classical in content. He would create the overall form and structure of a piece of furniture and Fornasetti would decorate its surfaces, often in highly surreal and exuberant *trompe-l'oeil* motifs. The humour and quirkiness of their work considerably influenced Italian design from 1960, not so much in applied decoration as in a general eccentricity of form and spirit; their designs can be seen as precursors of the anti-design movement which emerged during the 1960s and erupted in the 1980s through post-modernism.

Marco Zanuso (b. 1916), like Gio Ponti, was a multi-talented architect-designer who was accomplished in furniture, interior and industrial design. Commissioned by the Pirelli Company in 1948 to investigate the potential of foam rubber as a material for upholstery, he wrote, 'One could revolutionize not only the system of upholstery but also structural manufacturing and formal potential. When our prototypes acquired visually exciting and new contours, a company was founded to put models like the Lady into production with industrial standards that were previously unimaginable.'[9] This Lady chair won a gold medal at the ninth Milan Triennale of 1951. A sculptural and sophisticated design, it was produced by Arflex (established in March 1950), a branch of the huge Pirelli Company, as were other versions known as the Baby armchair and the Senior armchair. Arflex believed that furniture design had to make use of state-of-the-art manufacturing technology as well as current aesthetics. The success of both the company and Zanuso's furniture hinged on a close collaboration between designer and manufacturer. This type of working

Gio Ponti
Superleggera, 1957

53

relationship was also the key to Cassina's success with Gio Ponti, among others.

Franco Albini was the first architect-designer to work with Cassina and was highly influential in shaping the Italian Style. Albini trained as an architect at the Politecnico di Milano and while there gained knowledge of the rationalist design theories of the Bauhaus. During the 1930s he exhibited, as a rationalist, his furniture designs at the Monza Biennale exhibitions. Albini promoted rationalism throughout his working life and argued for 'the search for novelty for novelty's sake, unique pieces, simple and neat technical solutions to design problems, the promotion of mass-produced objects, and the proclivity for working with commonplace materials'.[10] His furniture designs express an uncomplicated modernism that derives from a natural sensitivity to materials and form. In 1952, he designed the Fiorenza chair for Arflex which was admired for its simple lines and exactness of form. George Nelson's remarks on postwar Italian rational design, made in 1948, were to prove just as apt a decade later: 'The best Italian works exude a seriousness, precision and drastic economy that makes them less quickly understandable. One needs a definite intellectual standard and understanding of modern design to appreciate the finesse and luxury of these Italian works.'[11]

With his brother Fulgenzio, architect-designer Osvaldo Borsani founded the furniture manufacturing company Tecno in 1952. Tecno mainly produced furniture for contract use and was established on the principle that design should be born out of research. Osvaldo explained: 'The experiments with outside designers have never brought satisfactory results, our products aren't the consequence of a sudden genial inspiration, but rather connected to one another; our collections have progressively extended and integrated with no sudden fancies.'[12] The majority of furniture produced by Tecno was designed by Osvaldo Borsani, who made full use of

newly developed materials, such as foam rubber. His greatest design success was the P40 chaise designed in 1954. Innovative in its use of foam-rubber upholstery and supported on an articulated steel frame, this handsome chaise-longue was highly flexible. Designed the same year, the D70 sofa, of similar construction to the P40, was fully reclinable through 180 degrees. The supreme functionalism of these two rational designs undoubtedly contributed to their great success.

Another family partnership was that of the Castiglioni brothers, Achille (b. 1918), Pier Giacomo (1913–68) and Livio (1911–79), who were extremely proficient designers primarily known for their lighting designs. The brothers practised within two different areas of design – mass production and limited production – and while they successfully designed for both categories of manufacturing, it was their limited-production furniture that created the most interest.

Achille and Pier Giacomo conceived several designs that they referred to as 'readymades', echoing the ideas that Marcel Duchamp (1887–1968) expressed with his artwork earlier in the century. Their Mezzadro (Sharecropper) stool of 1957 and Sgabello per Telefono (Telephone Stool) of the same year were regarded as so avant-garde that production of them could not be justified until 1970 and 1983 respectively. These 'ready-made' pieces of furniture consisted of existing mass-produced elements, such as tractor or bicycle seats, which were applied outside their usual context. The idiosyncratic nature of these designs was intended to dispel the public's preconceived notions of what a chair should look like. Like the anti-art philosophy of Dada, the work of the Castiglionis was anti-design.

It is not surprising that Dino Gavina – 'the most emotional and impulsive furniture manufacturer in the world',[13] according to Marcel Breuer – should have found the designs of the brothers appealing. Gavina was a close friend of Marcel Duchamp and the American Dadaist, Man Ray (1890–1977). Gavina's company manufactured the Lierna and Sanluca chairs designed by the Castiglioni brothers in 1958 and 1959. In this furniture, 'the convergence of the architect's brilliance and the commercial indifference of the manufacturer (who is first and foremost an aesthetic operator) is the basis for the remarkable construction of a figurative language, with powerful intonations, extraneous to the concept and practice of style'.[14] Achille and Pier Giacomo were both involved in the founding of the Italian A.D.I. awards and in 1954 helped organize the first Compasso d'Oro award. They had a direct influence on the next generation of designers, as both taught architecture and design at the Milan and Turin polytechnics.

Scandinavian furniture design thrived during the 1950s, evolving from its well-established foundations, which had been laid in the 1930s by designers such as Alvar Aalto and Bruno Mathsson and reinforced by Hans Wegner in the 1940s. With insufficient mechanization for large-scale mass production, most Scandinavian furniture in the early 1950s was still hand finished, relying on skilled craftsmen and natural materials; this solid wood furniture had wide international appeal, particularly in America and Germany. While much of the comfortable, practical furniture produced in Sweden at this time still relied on native woods, teak was the wood with which many Scandinavian designers – most especially the Danes – now preferred to work. Primarily imported from the Philippines, this superior hardwood had been logged during the Second World War as a result of road clearing. The subsequent surplus of teak was reasonably priced, and came to be so widely used that furniture by Finn Juhl (b. 1912), Arne Jacobsen (b. 1902), Hans Wegner, Borge Mogensen and Peter Hvidt has been labelled as Teak Style.

The Dane Hans Wegner continued to produce successful furniture designs throughout the decade. He possessed a great talent for both three-dimensional design and, just as importantly, cabinet-making. Linking design and craftsmanship, Wegner created furniture that embodied a purity and spiritual dignity, reminiscent of the Shaker aesthetic. His beautifully crafted Stacking chairs of 1951, though partly machine made, express this unity of design most eloquently.

Finn Juhl, also Danish, became an increasingly influential designer in the 1950s, winning international acclaim. Tribal art and contemporary organic sculpture inspired his use of lively, undulating forms carved from solid wood. Juhl explored the limits of this medium with the highest degree of craftsmanship and considered his work to be on a par with fine art. The virtuosity of his designs precluded the imitation that had beset so much 'Danish modern' furniture from the late 1940s onwards. In 1951, Juhl's furniture was manufactured in the United States, according to his specifications, by Barker. His teak armchair, of the same year, stands out as one of the best of these production designs and, not surprisingly, was included in the 'Good Design' exhibitions in New York and Chicago.

During the later years of the decade, Scandinavian avant-garde design altered course with the rise of a new generation of designers. Arne Jacobsen, Poul Kjaerholm (1929–80) and Verner Panton (b. 1926) looked to the work of Charles Eames and other American designers for inspiration and were attracted to the new methods of moulding plywood and, more importantly, fibreglass. Their furniture remained organic, but in form rather than in its use of materials. Like their predecessors, these designers believed in the truthful use of materials, despite the fact that they were now using synthetic resins and plastics.

Much of Arne Jacobsen's furniture was designed specifically for his own, highly integrated architectural briefs. For his best-known projects – the Scandinavian Airlines Terminal and the Royal Hotel, Copenhagen, both of 1958–60 – Jacobsen designed the Swan and Egg chairs. Using foam-upholstered, single-seat shell constructions, these two chairs were brilliantly original and organically sculptural in form. Unlike Eames and Saarinen, who had earlier used FRP (fibreglass-reinforced plastic) in their single-moulding processes, Jacobsen employed high-density, rigid

55

polyurethane foam for the seating shells. As celebrated as the Swan and Egg chairs were, his greatest commercial success was with a series of chairs based on the simple construction of a single moulded-plywood seat supported by three or four metal legs. Designed between 1951 and 1957, these chairs were available with natural oak, teak or rosewood veneers, coloured finishes or upholstery. Of the numerous variations that were mass-produced by Fritz Hansen, the Ant chair of 1952 was among the most popular. The success of Jacobsen's designs was due almost entirely to his rational approach to materials and production techniques combined, like Gio Ponti and Charles Eames, with a close collaborative relationship with the manufacturer.

Verner Panton, who was an associate of Arne Jacobsen, opened his own design office in Binningen, Switzerland, in 1955. Like Jacobsen, Panton believed that designers must make full use of new technology and materials: 'Steel tubes, foam, springs and covers have been so developed technically that we create forms which were unthinkable just a few years ago. Designers should now use materials to create objects which up to now they could only see in their dreams. Personally, I'd like to design chairs which exhaust all the technical possibilities of the present.'[15] His futuristic Cone and Heart chairs, designed in 1959, were the result of a conscious decision to divorce himself from any preconceived notions of how a chair should be designed. When conceptualizing a design, Panton concerned himself primarily with the inherent potential of new materials and their application. This approach, which by its very nature promotes unusual, forward-looking furniture, was to become increasingly important in the 1960s, influencing 'space age' designers such as Olivier Mourgue (b. 1939), Pierre Paulin and Geoffrey Harcourt (b. 1935).

At the end of the 1950s Panton was not the only designer determined to promote radical innovation in design, for although the economic recovery and subsequent boom in the 1950s created an unprecedented surge of consumerism, by the end of the decade it was becoming clear that the quality of much mass-produced furniture was undergoing a general decline. Mass production had necessitated a rational approach to design, but rationalism had led to a standardization that did not meet the needs of a consumer-based popular culture – a culture that would become increasingly demanding over the next few years. The British furniture industry, certainly, was reluctant to produce anything that was not guaranteed a safe niche in the broad home furnishings market, as Richard Hamilton described: 'There is too little stress laid on product design research in the consumer goods industries, too little initiation of product programmes at the design level, not enough probing of markets and too many curbs on imagination.'[16]

A related problem was the rise of kitsch: designs that were the result of months or years of research and investment were facing competition from a rash of feeble imitations. The Council of Industrial Design attempted to suppress this development in Britain, expressing concern over the decorative excesses prevalent in kitsch adulterations of contemporary 'high style' furniture. The Council began advocating a return to strict modernist principles – visual simplicity, restraint in the use of materials, functionalism – and granted awards only to designs that met these criteria.

In European and American furniture design in the late 1950s, therefore, the perceived failure of rationalism in a consumer-led society together with the widespread rise of kitsch led people to question the direction that design had taken. Even before 1960, innovative designers were searching for new forms of expression.

25 **Osvaldo Borsani**
P40, 1954

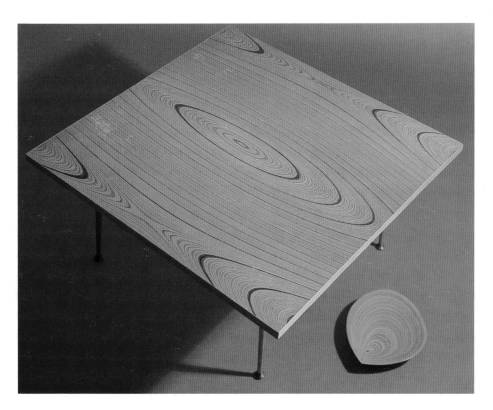

26 **Charles Eames**
RAR-1 rocking chair, 1950

27 **Tappio Wirkkala**
Table and dish, c. 1950

28 **Marco Zanuso**
    Lady sofa, 1951

29 **Marco Zanuso**
    Lady chairs, 1951

30 **L. B. Belgiojoso and E. Peressutti**
    Elettra chair, 1954

31 **Erberto Carboni**
    Delfino armchair, 1954

32 **William Katavolos, Ross Littell
    and Douglas Kelley**
    New York sofa, 1952

33 **Harry Bertoia**
    Wire side chair with child's
    chair, 1952

34 **Angelo Ostuni**
    Cross-frame table, 1956

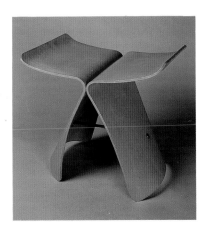

35 **Gio Ponti and Piero Fornasetti**
Bedroom for ninth Milan
Triennale, 1951

36 **Robert Heritage**
Sideboard, 1954

37 **Sori Yanagi**
Butterfly stool, 1956

38 **Charles Eames**
EA105 Aluminium Group side
chair, 1958

39 **George Nelson**
Kangaroo chair, 1956

40 **Charles Eames**
Lounge chair and ottoman, 1956

41 **Osvaldo Borsani**
D70 and P40, 1954

42 **Eero Saarinen**
    Tulip chair, 1957

43 **Estelle and Erwine Laverne**
    Daffodil chair, 1958

44 **Carlo Mollino**
Writing desk, 1950

45 **Silvio Cavatorta**
Desk, *c.* 1955

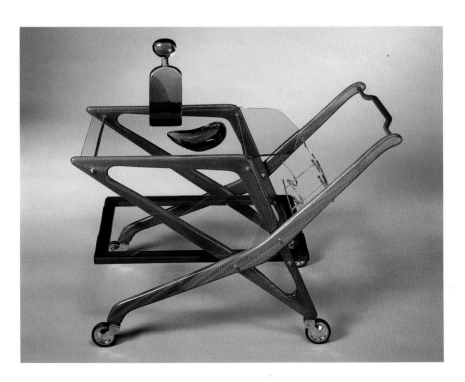

46 **Erwine and Estelle Laverne**
Lotus chair, 1958

Pierre Paulin
Desk, 1956–58 and lamp, 1955

47 **Cesare Lacca**
Trolley, *c.* 1955

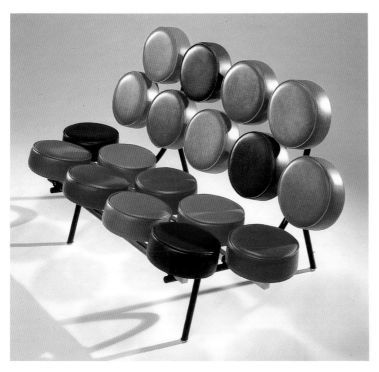

48 **Poul Kjaerholm**
PK22 chairs, 1957 (left), PK31
sofa, 1958 (centre) and PK24
chaise, 1965 (right)

49 **Francesco Aschieri**
Cabinet, 1956

50 **Piero Fornasetti**
Guitar and Sun chairs, c. 1955

51 **Arne Jacobsen**
3107 chairs, 1955

52 **George Nelson**
Marshmallow sofa, 1956

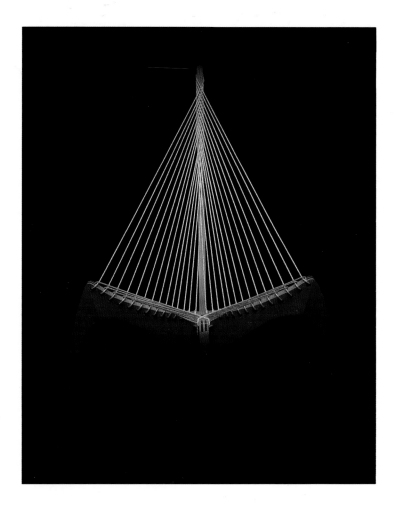

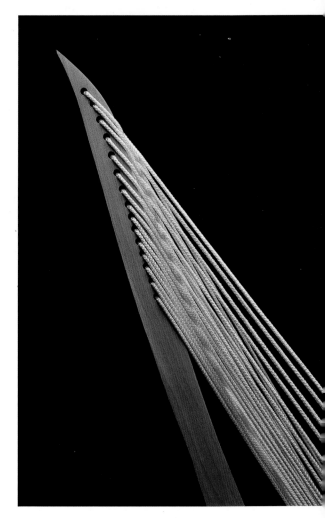

53 **Jørgen Hovelskov**
Harp chair, 1958

54 **Jørgen Hovelskov**
Harp chair, 1958 (detail)

55 **Verner Panton**
Cone chair, 1959

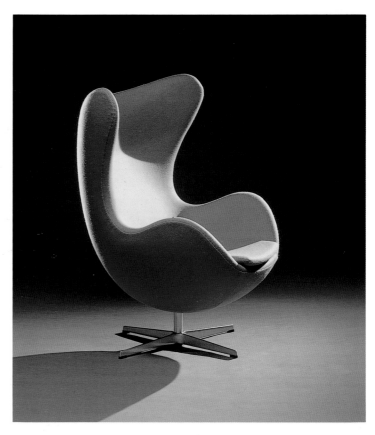

56 **Paul Goldman**
    Cherner armchair, 1957

57 **Arne Jacobsen**
    Egg chair, 1957

58 **Verner Panton**
    Cone chairs (upholstered), 1959

59 **Pierre Paulin**
    437 Easy armchairs, 1959

Eero Saarinen designed the Pedestal Chair for Knoll Associates.
See it at the Museum of Modern Art in New York or
Knoll Showrooms in 28 countries.

Knoll Associates, Inc., Furniture and Textiles, 320 Park Avenue, New York, New York 10022.

60 **Eero Saarinen**
    Tulip chair in Knoll
    International advertisement,
    c. 1960

61 **Eero Saarinen**
    Tulip Pedestal Group, 1957

Notes on the furniture

Osvaldo Borsani, Italian, b. 1911

P40, 1954* (25)
Tecno, Italy

Pressed steel frame upholstered in jersey-covered latex-foam with steel spring-lined rubber armrests

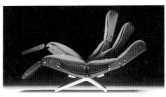

25

The P40 has an articulated frame which can be adjusted into 486 positions. The foot rest is retractable and the arm rests, which form parabolic curves, can be pushed down. It has been described as 'a machine for sitting, of the greatest sophistication' (*see Modern Chairs*, exhibition catalogue, Whitechapel Art Gallery, London 1971, page 116).

Charles Eames, American, 1907–78

RAR-1 rocking chair, 1950 (26)
Herman Miller Inc., USA

Vinyl-upholstered, moulded fibreglass-reinforced plastic seat shell on a steel rod base attached to solid wood rockers

26

The RAR-1 is part of the Plastic Armchair Group developed between 1950 and 1953 by Eames and Zenith Plastics of Gardena, California. Originally, the chairs' plastic shells were available in grey, grey-green and beige, but in 1951 a greater choice of colours and upholstered versions was introduced. There were over fifteen variations, including the DAR dining chair, the LAR lounge chair and a swivelling version on castors.

Tappio Wirkkala, Finnish, b. 1915

Table and dish, *c*. 1950 (27)
Soinne et Kni, Finland

Laminated birch bowl and table top on metal legs

27

Wirkkala exhibited at the Milan Triennale of 1951, where he was awarded a Grand Prix for this dish.

Marco Zanuso, Italian, b. 1916

Lady sofa, 1951 (28)
Arflex, Italy

Metal frame with fabric-covered, foam-rubber upholstery, on tubular metal legs

In 1948 Zanuso was commissioned by Pirelli to explore the viability of foam rubber for upholstery; this sophisticated design was produced by Arflex.

28

29

Marco Zanuso, Italian, b. 1916

Lady chairs, 1951* (29)
Arflex, Italy

Metal frame with fabric-covered, foam-rubber upholstery, on tubular metal legs

Zanuso won a gold medal for his Lady chair at the 1951 Milan Triennale.

Lodovico Barbiano di Belgiojoso, Italian, b. 1909 and **Enrico Peressutti**, Italian, 1908–75

Elettra chair, 1954* (30)
Arflex, Italy

30

Tubular metal frame upholstered in foam rubber with fabric covering

Like Zanuso, the design group known as BBPR exploited the potential of foam-rubber upholstery. The fact that bulky spring constructions were no longer necessary led to more economical and sculptural forms. Arflex was at the forefront of this seating revolution.

Erberto Carboni, Italian

Delfino armchair, 1954*(31)
Arflex, Italy

Tubular metal frame with fabric-covered, foam-rubber upholstery

The Delfino, Carboni's best-known furniture design, had a matching ottoman.

31

32

William Katavolos, American, b. 1924, **Ross Littell**, American, b. 1924 and **Douglas Kelley**, American, b. 1928

New York sofa, 1952*(32)
Cadsana, Italy

Leather-covered, foam-upholstered metal frame on chromium-plated metal legs with black enamelled metal stretchers

The New York sofa, or 7FC, is part of the New Furniture Group, which was initially manufactured by Laverne Originals, USA. The 3LC or 'T' chair was the most acclaimed design of this series.

Harry Bertoia, American (born in Italy), 1915–78

Wire side chair with child's chair, 1952*
Knoll International, USA (33)

33

Hand bent and welded steel-rod construction, either chromium-plated or with nylon paint finish

The metal rods used in the construction of these chairs were bent by hand – the most efficient and cost-effective method.

Angelo Ostuni, Italian

Cross-frame table, 1956 (34)
Frangi, Italy

34

Solid walnut frame supporting a glass top

Ostuni's sophisticated and beautifully crafted designs are typical of limited-production furniture from small Italian workshops during this period.

Gio Ponti, Italian, 1891–1979 and **Piero Fornasetti**, Italian, 1913–88

Bedroom for ninth Milan Triennale, 1951
Gio Ponti and Piero Fornasetti, Italy (35)

Laminated wood construction with screenprinted decoration

This extraordinary bed and wardrobe are in the Bischofberger Collection, Zurich.

35

Robert Heritage, British, b. 1927

Sideboard, 1954
A.G. Evans, UK

36

Metal-rod legs supporting solid wood carcase with ebonized top and sides and screenprinted, birch-veneered doors

The dramatic contrast between the birch-veneered and the ebonized elements is unusual for UK case furniture of this date.

Sori Yanagi, Japanese, b. 1915

Butterfly stool, 1956 (37)
Tendo Mokko, Japan

Moulded plywood elements joined with
metal stretcher and screws

The highly organic Butterfly stool could be
easily dismantled for transportation and
was very well received in America.

37

38

Charles Eames, American, 1907–78

EA105 Aluminium Group side chair, 1958*
Herman Miller Inc., USA (38)

Vinyl-covered latex foam-upholstered sling
attached to aluminium frame on a four-
point pedestal base

Known during its development as the
Leisure Group or Indoor-Outdoor Group,
the Aluminium Group currently comprises
a high-back, tilt-swivel lounge chair, a low-
and high-back, tilt-swivel desk chair with
an adjustable seat and a low-back side chair
(all with or without arms) as well as an
ottoman, a coffee table and a dining table
available with a variety of tops. Originally
intended for domestic retail, the group was
eventually marketed for contract use. A
cool tone, warm tone and eggplant gloss
finishes are now available.

George Nelson, American, 1907–86

Kangaroo chair, 1956
Herman Miller Inc., USA

39

Upholstered, moulded-plywood shell with
latex foam-filled seat and back cushions, on
a chromium-plated steel frame

Although less innovative in form than other
designs by Nelson Associates such as the

Coconut chair, the Kangaroo chair was
perhaps more functional. Relatively light in
weight, the Kangaroo chair, like Eames'
Lounge chair of the same year, alluded to
traditional English club chairs with the
buttoning of its cushion.

Charles Eames, American, 1907–78

Lounge chair and ottoman, 1956* (40)
Herman Miller Inc., USA

Cast-aluminium, five-point swivelling
pedestal base supporting rosewood-
veneered, moulded-plywood seat and back
shells, with leather-covered foam-rubber
and down-filled, buttoned upholstery

40

With the Lounge chair 670 and matching
ottoman 671, Eames' intention to effect the
'warm receptive look of a well-used first
baseman's mitt' (*see* Neuhart, Neuhart and
Eames, *Eames Design*, New York 1989,
page 207) was achieved through the use of
buttoning, which intentionally held the
leather's surface creases. Originally
conceived as a gift for Billy Wilder, the
chair was thought to be destined for a short
production run – it was relatively
expensive, retailing at $634.00 in 1957 – but
it became one of the company's greatest
retail successes.

Osvaldo Borsani, Italian, b. 1911

D70 and P40, 1954
Tecno, Italy

41

Both with pressed-steel frames upholstered
in jersey-covered latex-foam, the P40 with
steel spring-lined rubber armrests

The D70 and P40 were designed to meet the
demand for multi-purpose furniture; both
had contract and domestic applications.

Eero Saarinen, American (born in Finland),
1910–61

Tulip chair, 1957* (42)
Knoll International, USA

Plastic-coated, cast-aluminium pedestal base supporting a moulded, fibreglass-reinforced plastic seat shell, with fabric-covered, latex foam-upholstered cushion

Part of the Pedestal Group, which Saarinen designed in 1956, this particular example of the Tulip chair was produced in 1957.

Estelle Laverne, American, b. 1915 and
Erwine Laverne, American, b. 1909

Daffodil chair, 1958 (43)
Laverne International, USA

Moulded perspex seat shell and base with fabric-covered, foam-filled seat cushion

The Daffodil chair formed part of the Invisible Group launched in 1957, although this example was produced in 1958.

Carlo Mollino, Italian, 1905–73

Writing desk, 1950 (44)
Istituto Cooperazione Sanitaria, Italy

Solid wood drawer unit and free-form security plate-glass top, supported by a moulded and perforated plywood frame with further single drawer unit attached

Commissioned for the Singer Store in Turin, this is similar to the earlier Reale desk (*see* colour plate 6) in that it has a hanging drawer unit to one side and a separate single drawer unit.

Silvio Cavatorta, Italian, b. 1890s

Desk, *c.* 1955 (45)
Silvio Cavatorta, Italy

Solid oak construction

This desk was designed by Silvio Cavatorta in association with his more famous son, Franco, and was manufactured in the family workshop specifically for the office of Enrico Mattei, President of the ENI Group. The desk, with a matching chair, is now in the Manchester City Art Galleries' twentieth-century study collection.

Erwine Laverne, American, b. 1909 and
Estelle Laverne, American, b. 1915

Lotus chair, 1958 (46)
Laverne International, USA

Fibreglass-reinforced plastic moulded seat shell supported on a four-point aluminium pedestal base

The elegant Lotus echoes in spirit the Lavernes' Invisible chairs of 1957.

Pierre Paulin, French, b. 1927

Desk, 1956–58 and **lamp**, 1955 (46)
Thonet, France

Solid oak drawer unit with black formica top supported on enamelled metal frame

The geometric functionalism of this early desk by Paulin is quite different from the sculptural elegance of his 1960s work. The lamp, made by Phillips, The Netherlands, has a solid brass stand supporting a pierced, black-enamelled metal shade.

Cesare Lacca, Italian
Trolley, *c.* 1955 (47)
Cesare Lacca, Italy

47

Plate-glass shelves supported by a solid mahogany frame with brass mounts and castors

In the 1950s Lacca produced several elegant solid wood tables and trolleys.

Poul Kjaerholm, Danish, 1929–80

PK22 chairs, 1957,* **PK31 sofa**, 1958* and **PK24 chaise**, 1965* (48)
Fritz Hansen, Denmark

PK22, stainless-steel frame supporting woven cane seat; PK31, stainless-steel frame supporting leather-covered, upholstered seat and back; PK24, stainless-steel frame supporting cane seat and back with goat-skin covered headrest

48

Kjaerholm's furniture was included in several Milan Triennales and in 1957 and 1960 these designs were awarded the Grand Prix. The PK24 or Hammock chair was originally manufactured by E. Kold Christensen, Copenhagen before Fritz Hansen took over production in the 1970s. The cane seats of PK22 and PK24 are handwoven, making them expensive to manufacture.

Francesco Aschieri, Italian

Cabinet, 1956
Mensio, Italy

49

Copper legs supporting a plywood construction with screen-printed decoration and copper-mounted glass shelves

The screen-printed decoration of fish and flora on this cabinet was inspired by the work of artists such as Hans Arp. The

exaggerated use of applied decoration and asymmetrical forms resulted in a plethora of kitsch imitations in the late 1950s.

Piero Fornasetti, Italian, 1913–88

Guitar and Sun chairs, *c.* 1955* (50)
Fornasetti, Italy

Black-enamelled, tubular metal legs (originally solid wood) supporting a moulded plywood seat with lacquered and screen-printed decoration

These chairs have been offered in various colour combinations of black and white, or orange, yellow and black, and occasionally with a negative image.

50

51

Arne Jacobsen, Danish, 1902–71

3107 chairs, 1955* (51)
Fritz Hansen, Denmark

Moulded plywood seat supported on satin chromium-plated, tubular steel legs

At the 1957 Milan Triennale, a Grand Prix was awarded to the 3107 or Series 7 chairs. Five different models included an armchair and a swivelling office chair. The chairs are available with face veneers of oak, rosewood and teak as well as in various colours, with an ebonized finish or upholstered. Jacobsen also designed a linking device so that the chairs could be clipped into rows for auditorium use.

George Nelson, American, 1907–86

Marshmallow sofa, 1956 (52)
Herman Miller Inc., USA

Vinyl-covered, latex-foam cushions on a black-enamelled tubular steel frame

52

Only a few hundred Marshmallow sofas were produced (1956–63). Available with fabric, vinyl or leather coverings, the shocking pink, orange and purple vinyl combination illustrated was among the most popular. With this sofa, Nelson Associates suggested that rationally conceived design could be characterized by eccentricity and humour rather than utility and sobriety. Designed primarily for contract use, this sofa predicted the direction domestic furniture design would take in the 1960s.

Jørgen Hovelskov, Danish

Harp chair, 1958 (53,54)
Jørgen Christensens Snedkeri, Denmark

Solid birch frame strung with flag line

The shape of the Harp chair was based on the bow section of early Viking sailing vessels. This maritime influence was emphasized by the seat support system, which comprised a strung flag line resembling nautical rigging. Although light in appearance the chair is very stable.

Verner Panton, Danish, b. 1926

Cone chair, 1959*(55)
Fritz Hansen, Denmark

Bent chromium-plated or black-enamelled steel rod construction with fabric-covered latex foam seat and back cushions on swivelling circular pedestal base

Panton has been acclaimed for producing, 'innovative designs based on iconoclastic thinking' (*see* Ann Lee Morgan, *Contemporary Designers*, 1985, page 469). In the construction of the earlier Cone chairs, a metal four-point pedestal base was used rather than the current circular configuration.

Paul Goldman, American, b. 1912

Cherner armchair, 1957 (56)
Plycraft, USA

Moulded plywood with walnut or birch face veneers

The Cherner armchair and matching side chair were offered with or without upholstery and a two-tone veneered variation was also available. These designs were a direct outcome of Goldman's wartime research into advanced moulded plywood technology and his interest in boat building.

Arne Jacobsen, Danish, 1902–71

Egg chair, 1957*(57)
Fritz Hansen, Denmark

Tilting and swivelling cast-aluminium, four-point pedestal base supporting fabric-covered, latex foam-upholstered, moulded fibreglass-reinforced polyurethane shell with loose seat cushion

The upholstery of the Egg chair 3316 and matching ottoman 3127 is glued to the moulded plastic shell and then tightly covered in fabric, vinyl or leather.

Verner Panton, Danish, b. 1926

Cone chairs (upholstered), 1959 (58)
Fritz Hansen, Denmark

Four-point cast-aluminium swivelling pedestal base supporting a fabric or vinyl-upholstered, bent sheet metal construction with latex-foam seat cushion

Panton's upholstered Cone chair was smaller than the wire rod version. Its futuristic shape was partly a result of his quest, like that of Saarinen, for a unified form: 'The result rarely has four legs' (*see* C. and K. Fehrman, *Postwar Interior Design: 1945–1960*, New York 1987, page 82).

58

Pierre Paulin, French, b. 1927

437 Easy armchairs, 1959* (59)
Artifort, The Netherlands

Chromium-plated tubular metal frame supporting jersey-covered, foam-upholstered, moulded plywood seat and back

The 437 Easy armchair is available in a variety of coloured textiles.

59

Eero Saarinen, American (born in Finland), 1910–61

Tulip chair in Knoll International advertisement, *c.* 1960 (60)

This advertisement is one of a series that appeared in *Fortune* and *The New Yorker*; one of the responses Knoll received was from a man inquiring where he could obtain the model's silver skirt for his wife.

60

61

Eero Saarinen, American (born in Finland), 1910–61

Tulip Pedestal Group, 1957* (61)
Knoll International, USA

Plastic-coated, cast-aluminium pedestal bases supporting moulded, fibreglass-reinforced plastic seat shells with fabric-covered, latex foam-upholstered cushions

The Pedestal Group consists of an armchair, side chair, two stools and several tables with a selection of marble, wooden and plastic-laminated tops.

1960 to 1970   Pop culture and anti-design

Mario Bellini
Teneride, c. 1968

Vico Magistretti
Selene chairs, 1961

Olivier Mourgue
Djinn chaise-longue, 1963

3

The period 1960 to 1970
was a time of social and political
unrest. Nothing was sacrosanct;
everything was open to examination
and reform. New ideas and aspirations
were widely disseminated throughout
society by the mass media and, in
particular, television. This was the
twilight period of booming
consumerism before the oil crisis and
economic recession of the early 1970s.
Public enthusiasm for the enormous
variety and volume of industrial output
had never been higher. As a result of
increased demand and huge advances
in communications, the furniture
market became truly international.

Avant-garde furniture designers in
the 1960s generally renounced any
former predilection for exclusive, high-
quality designs produced in small
numbers and displayed a new
commitment to designs intended for
high-volume, mass consumption.
Major manufacturers by 1960 were
concentrating almost entirely on the
contract market; indeed, the new
decade saw the progressive
development of pure contract design
that possessed virtually no domestic
value. In response to the vacuum that
this created in the domestic home
furnishings market and in opposition
to the rationalism which promoted the
durability of function and aesthetics,
the avant-garde moved towards a
consumer-oriented style that embraced
popular culture.

By the early part of the decade, the
postwar baby boom had initiated a
shift of emphasis within the mass
market, leading it to become
significantly more youth-based, while
an upsurge in social mobility led to a
dramatic liberalization of social and
moral values, creating a new pluralism
in both taste and design. An anti-
materialist *Zeitgeist* encouraged people
to reject the traditional association of
furniture with permanance, high cost
and status; what was required by the
growing market of younger consumers
was unpretentious, low-cost furniture
that would be reflective of a liberal-
minded and classless society.

The furniture industry was receptive
to these new demands and took
advantage of the low world price of oil,

making full use of low-cost petroleum by-products such as plastics. Just as plywood and FRP had been the materials of the 1950s, ABS (Acrylonitrile Butadiene Styrene), polyethylene and other thermoplastics were the materials of the 1960s. These advanced synthetic compounds did not need to be reinforced and were therefore light in weight. They were also extremely strong, could be easily coloured and possessed a high-gloss surface on both sides. Although the new plastics were inexpensive, tooling up moulds for them was costly, so manufacturers employed relatively large production runs. This meant that they had either to create a static product line of high-quality, rationally designed furniture that would be mainly aimed at the contract market, or develop continuously changing, short-lived yet high-volume production runs of affordable furniture that was dependent on fashion and novelty value. By 1960, the concept of built-in obsolescence in both materials and aesthetics was generally accepted by designers, particularly in America, as it increased production and was therefore believed to be beneficial to the economy. British artist Richard Hamilton put forward the assets of this theory in a lecture at the Institute of Contemporary Arts in London, but the Council of Industrial Design remained reluctant to put it into practice. In America, the preoccupation with 'lifestyle' – designing the consumers to fit the products – was one of the key elements in the creation of Pop culture. As critic Reyner Banham wrote in 1963: 'The aesthetics of Pop depend on a massive initial impact and small sustaining power and are therefore at their poppiest in products whose sole object is to be consumed.'[1] This approach to design, that is, one that stressed the importance of consumer sales and changing fashions, marks the primary difference between furniture from the 1950s and 1960s.

Pop culture led furniture designers to explore the potential of anti-design – also known as counter design – which challenged one of the principal tenets of the Modern Movement, that is, the inherent value of functionalism. In the 1950s, design had been dominated by functionalism, but by the early 1960s the booming consumer culture encouraged individualism rather than standardization. The debate surrounding the dichotomy of functionalism and mass consumerism grew in intensity and became internationally widespread. Abraham Moles was a lecturer at a design school that was founded on the principles of the Modern Movement – indeed, its first rector was Max Bill, a former Bauhaus student – the Hochschule für Gestaltung (1955–68) in Ulm, in what was then West Germany. As Moles stated in 1967: 'Functionalism necessarily contradicts the doctrine of an affluent society which is forced to produce and sell relentlessly . . . . [it] tends to reduce the number of objects and to realize an optimal fit between products and needs, whereas the production machinery of an affluent society follows the opposite direction. It creates a system of neokitsch by accumulating objects in the human environment. At this point the crisis of functionalism becomes manifest. It is torn between the neokitsch of the supermarket on the one side and ascetic fulfilment of function on the other.'[2]

It was accepted, however, that in order to increase furniture production, designers would have to make use of state-of-the-art technology. Polypropylene had been invented by Giulio Natta in 1954 and as a thermoplastic, it was highly suited to the latest injection moulding processes. Robin Day realized that this new material would be ideal for low-cost, mass-produced seating. As design director of Hille, Day had already advised the company to buy the British rights to produce the Eameses' designs, including the 1948 fibreglass chair, the DAR. In 1963, recognizing the potential of polypropylene, Day set about designing a chair that would make full use of the plastic's exceptional properties. The result was the Polypropylene chair, which was without doubt the most successful British contract design of the decade. At the time of the chair's launch, the *Architect's Journal* considered: 'This excellent solution to the multipurpose

Roger Dean
Sea Urchin, 1968

side chair will certainly prove to be the most significant development in British mass-produced design since the war.'[3]

Domestic furniture design, meanwhile, was being increasingly influenced by Pop culture. In 1963 *The Sunday Times Magazine* published an article criticizing the 'good taste' of contemporary Scandinavian design: 'For years Scandinavia has been the dominating influence on our furniture and furnishings. We have come to accept mass-produced perfection . . . . What we need is an unexpected touch of salt; something not off the conveyor belt.'[4] It was becoming apparent to the younger generation of designers that the public was bored with rationally designed products. The new consumers believed that fashion was more important than function and they no longer required 'definitive' design solutions but a continuum of inexpensive, expendable products.

That Pop culture was so well established in Britain in the early 1960s was due partly to the efforts made by a group of progressive artists and critics in the previous decade. The Independent Group, formed in 1952, set out to examine the technical achievements of American industry and the early emergence of popular culture in the United States. The group, which included Richard Hamilton, Eduardo Paolozzi, Reyner Banham, and Peter and Alison Smithson, rejected modernist philosophy. Hamilton identified the characteristics of Pop art as, 'Popular (designed for a mass audience), Transient (short-term solution), Expendable (easily forgotten), Low Cost, Mass Produced, Young (aimed at Youth), Witty, Sexy, Gimmicky, Glamorous, Big Business.'[5] Pop essentially drew inspiration from 'low' art rather than 'high' art and was raised to a topic of serious academic interest by the Independent Group through seminars and discussions.

The movement towards a new popular culture was given further encouragement in 1961, when a number of English architects, including Michael Webb, Peter Cook, Dennis Crompton and Ron Herron, formed the design group Archigram. It was primarily concerned with architectural projects for futuristic cities and 'megastructures' that were never intended to be realized. The schemes, such as Sin City, Plug-in City and Walking City, represented an exploration of the fantastic, but were rationally conceived within the constraints of what their creators believed to be a future reality. Their complex city planning consisted of long-term shell structures, which could be filled with expendable living, office and shop units; the concept of capsule homes was supposed to allow architecture to become a truly popular consumer product. The group stated: 'A new generation of architecture must arise with forms and spaces which seem to reject the precepts of "Modern" yet in fact retain these precepts. WE HAVE CHOSEN TO BY-PASS THE DECAYING BAUHAUS IMAGE WHICH IS AN INSULT TO FUNCTIONALISM.'[6] The proposition that anti-design could be more rational than 'good design' in a consumer-led society became the single most important design debate of the decade.

In 1963, Peter Murdoch (b. 1940) designed his Child's chair, which was decorated with a colourful Pop art-inspired pattern. This innovative chair was constructed of a single sheet of polyethylene-coated, laminated paperboard and was sold in flat-pack form. The Child's chair and the later, similarly constructed, Those Things chair, table and stool, were superb products, for they were designed specifically for mass consumption, possessed an immediate visual appeal, were inexpensive to manufacture and retailed at low cost. Even Paul Reilly, head of the Design Council, acknowledged the 'challenge of pop' and realized that 'in this age of accelerating technology, to refuse to take notice of the transitory or to reject the ephemeral *per se* is to ignore a fact of life'.[7] As a result of this reluctant acceptance of popular consumerism and anti-design, Murdoch's Child's chair received a Council of Industrial Design Award in 1968, evidently to the horror of the Duke of Edinburgh, who presented the prize. Murdoch's chair was designed to last for only a short time, and he was not the only British

83

designer to promote such furniture: in 1966, Bernard Holdaway designed the Tom-O-Tom dining table and chairs, which were constructed of a combination of chipboard and paper. Disposable paper furniture is perhaps one of the greatest symbols of consumerism. Murdoch and Holdaway pointed out that furniture design did not have to take itself seriously; it could be cheap, novel, fashionable, disposable and – most of all – fun.

The gimmicky quality of popular furniture design during this period was nurtured by the press: in February 1962, the first British colour supplement magazine was published by *The Sunday Times*, followed by the *Sunday Telegraph* in 1964 and the *Observer* in 1965. The first 'Design for Living' feature in *The Sunday Times* colour supplement in April 1962 insisted: 'Poor design has become a target for anyone with a brick to throw: good design is treated as a sort of sacred cow. The attitude to function is racing to the same level of absurdity . . . . There are times when one longs to buy something plumb ugly and utterly unfunctional.'[8] These sentiments must have sounded to the Council of Industrial Design like mutiny; it still firmly believed that by promoting the tenets of rationalism, society as a whole would benefit. The public had been starved of ornament in furniture design throughout the years of austerity and it now demanded colourful decoration and above all, greater consumer choice. Not surprisingly, there was a return to historicism, with, for example, a revival of elements of Art Nouveau. Against this bewildering backdrop of eclecticism – which included William Morris textile designs reproduced in psychedelic hues – it was generally acknowledged that modernism had reached a new low in popularity.

Modular furniture became increasingly popular in the 1960s. Max Clendenning's 1966 Maxima range consisted of twenty-five plywood elements that could be used to make up nearly three hundred permutations of furniture, including chairs, sofas, tables and wall units. Although relatively expensive, this 'Transformation Furniture' was highly successful, more because of its novelty than its flexibility. 'Knockdown' or 'flat-pack' furniture was highly favoured by consumers because it could be purchased and easily transported to the home for assembly on the same day. Retail outlets such as Habitat were founded on this new furniture-retailing concept; design was now a truly popular consumer 'product' that could be bought literally off the shelf.

Italian manufacturers realized that the only way to stay competitive with developments in Britain and America was to invest heavily in research, so designers were given studios and access to craftsmen and technicians, allowing them to develop a continuous stream of prototypes. These 'concept factories' accelerated advances in production techniques and new furniture types.

Italian manufacturers embraced popular culture and augmented already large and diverse product ranges. During this period of continuing economic growth, many new companies were formed and existing firms – including C & B, Kartell, Poltronova, Artemide and Zanotta – underwent expansion. Because of the large investment required for increased mechanization, manufacturers in Italy tended to specialize in specific areas of technology and subcontract out to other producers any part of the production process for which they did not possess the skills or machinery. Italian industry's greatest technical contribution to the 1960s was the advancement of injection moulding. During the war years and the 1950s, through the proliferation of mass production, the aesthetic standing of plastic had been downgraded; goods manufactured in synthetic materials were often poorly designed and were seen as cheap, throwaway products. In the 1960s, designers such as Vico Magistretti (b. 1920), Marco Zanuso and Joe Colombo (1930–71) were instrumental in returning plastic to its prewar status.

Until the late 1950s, it was only possible to produce small objects in thermoplastics, but in 1961 the Child's stacking chair was conceived by Richard Sapper (b. 1932) and Marco

Zanuso and was the earliest design intended for production in polyethylene. First produced in 1964, it was manufactured in component form with moulded grooves, in order to economize on materials. Zanuso wrote of polyethylene: 'This new material, in turn, led to the rethinking of the formal and structural characteristics of the chair . . . we had created a chair that was also a toy, which would stimulate a child's fantasy . . . . At the same time it was indestructible, and soft enough that it could not harm anyone yet too heavy to be thrown.'[9] In 1964, in recognition of the design's innovative use of plastics, the Child's chair was awarded a Compasso d'Oro.

Like Zanuso, Vico Magistretti promoted rationalism; the graceful Selene chair of 1961, which embodies his design philosophy, was originally produced in hot-pressed fibreglass, but in 1967 was manufactured in polyethylene by Artemide. The purity of this sleek design derives from Magistretti's fundamental understanding and rational use of thermoplastics' properties. As he suggested: 'However attractive we may find the post-modernist slogan (a strictly pro-styling slogan) "less is a bore", we may well come to believe that Mies got it right in thinking the best guarantee of durable quality lay in "less is more". I think perhaps the time has come to say; first we thought that what was useful was beautiful, but now we know that what is beautiful is useful.'[10] The enduring success of Magistretti's work lies in the delicate balance he is able to strike between functionalism and aesthetics; he is, without question, one of the greatest champions of late twentieth-century modernism.

Throughout his short career, Joe Colombo originated fresh furniture types. He is best known for his plastic furniture, such as the Elda armchair of 1963 – which was the first large armchair produced in fibreglass – and the 4867 Universale stacking chair designed in 1965.

During the later part of the decade, the idea of designing complete living spaces was very popular among the younger generation of Italian architect-designers and Joe Colombo's extensive work in this area resulted in some of his most exciting designs. In many ways his design tenet can be seen as a return to the prewar modernist approach, which promoted complete architectural schemes: 'All the objects in a house should be integrated with the usable spaces; hence they no longer ought to be called furnishings but "equipment".'[11] Colombo's designs are imbued with a belief in a future where mankind and technology would coexist in complete concordance. Much of his work was futuristic and utopian in spirit; this period marked the height of the American space programme and it is not surprising that the future was thought of in space-age terms. Colombo's Visiona Habitat or Total Furnishing Unit of 1969 was conceived as though it were a space station, with areas designated specific functions, such as the Night Cell or the Kitchen Box. Although highly sculptural, it was supremely efficient and incorporated many types of space- and labour-saving devices; furnishing systems were consolidated in the overall design, replacing individual pieces of furniture. This move towards integrated furnishings was influenced by traditional Japanese interior design.

Ettore Sottsass Jr. (b. 1917), like Colombo, was of the generation that bridged the gap between the pioneers of postwar Italian design and the new wave designers such as Andrea Branzi (b. 1938) and Alessandro Mendini (b. 1931). Sottsass was overwhelmingly regarded as a master designer by the younger generation, some of whom would work with him for Memphis in the early 1980s. He began his career in the 1950s as a product designer in the modernist tradition for Olivetti, but by the early 1960s was drawing inspiration from the anti-design objectives of Pop. His first non-rationalist designs were ceramic objects, although later he experimented with plastic laminates and in the mid-1960s began creating anti-design furniture for Poltronova. These first explorations by Ettore Sottsass into counter design can be seen as the foundations on which post-modernism in the decorative arts would be built.

Joe Colombo
Additional Living System, 1968

85

One of the greatest Italian exponents of 'radical' or anti-design during the 1960s was Gaetano Pesce (b. 1939), who was highly influenced by the work of American Pop artists, especially Claes Oldenburg. He explored the potential of new polyurethane-foam moulding techniques developed at the laboratories of C & B (Cassina & Buselli), a subsidiary of Cassina. His Up Series, designed in 1969, consisted of seven chairs with simple sculptural forms and bold colours and was promoted with a revolutionary marketing strategy: the chairs – apart from Up7, which was shaped as an enormous foot – were compressed to a tenth of their normal size and vacuum packed into boxes which, when opened, allowed the polyurethane-foam designs literally to bounce into life. This 'mutation', as Pesce put it, transformed the acquisition of furniture into a 'happening'. The Up Series established an international reputation for Pesce as a challenging, avant-garde architect-designer.

Several anti-design groups were founded during the decade, the most significant being Archizoom, Superstudio, UFO, Gruppo Strum and 9999. Though outside the industrial mainstream, these organizations enabled designers to interact with each other in the search for new forms of furniture inspired by Pop culture.

Archizoom, formed in 1966 by Andrea Branzi, Paolo Deganello (b. 1940), Gilberto Corretti and Massimo Morozzi (b. 1941), drew its name from the British design group, Archigram (which would be disbanded in 1974) and an issue of its journal entitled 'Zoom'. The most notable architectural projection Archizoom created was No-Stop City, a futuristic, never-ending urban environment which took rationalism to its ultimate conclusion. It designed the city without constraints in an effort to reveal that, if taken too far, rationalism becomes absurd, a point made by Branzi: 'Criticism of the Modern Movement was also and above all expressed by taking Rationalism to an extreme, with the intention of exposing the underlying contradictions of the movement, along with the fragile

nature of its apparent unity of research. It was no coincidence that Archizoom Associati wrote at the time: "The ultimate aim of modern architecture is the elimination of architecture itself." And the No-Stop City was nothing but the furthest outpost of Rationalism, reached by pushing all the data of the project to the point of paradox, almost in hyper-realistic fashion; the elimination of any striving for quality led towards an architecture that was all function, to the point of its being swallowed up by the latter.'[12]

Archizoom produced a number of significant furniture designs, including the Superonda of 1966, the Safari of 1968 and the Mies chair of 1969. The Superonda sofa possesses great visual impact and epitomizes Pop design, with its sculptural wave form covered in gleaming vinyl. It was not intended to be particularly functional, but rather was to be seen as a fashion statement that would survive only as long as the vogue lasted. Its polyurethane-foam structure was cheap to produce as it did not require expensive tooling. The Safari 'livingscape' design can be seen as the epitome of camp: this anti-design was presented, tongue in cheek, by Archizoom as, 'An imperial piece within the sordidness of your own home . . . a beautiful piece that you simply don't deserve. Clear out your lounges! Clear out your own lives as well!'[13] Like Archizoom's Dream beds of 1967, the Safari represents a vehement attack on 'good' taste. The Mies chair, however, is perhaps Archizoom's most blatant assault on rationalist design theory. Although the chair appears totally unfunctional with its extreme angularity and lack of upholstery, it is, in fact, surprisingly comfortable. Archizoom's ridiculing of a modernist designer through the Mies chair predicts the 'redesign' work of Alessandro Mendini and Studio Alchymia in the late 1970s.

Superstudio was founded by Adolfo Natalini, Cristano Toraldo di Francia, Gian Pietro Frassinelli and Roberto and Alessandro Magris with the aim of questioning the validity of rationalism in design and, specifically, in urban planning. It was highly critical of advanced technology and consumerism

Wendell Castle
Molar sofa, 1969–70

and urged for the 'design of evasion'; design that is industrially produced, yet poetic and irrational. Their provocative projections of 'super structures' and 'super' architectural grid systems, such as Continuous Monument, pointed to a dream-like world without consumer products where only monuments and unfunctional auto-destructing architecture existed. Superstudio's main contribution to furniture design was the Quaderna series of tables designed in 1969. Produced by Zanotta, the rectilinear tables were screen-printed with a continuous grid pattern and were consciously neutral in content.

Archizoom and Superstudio were both founded in Florence in 1966 and in the same year the city suffered the worst flooding of the Arno in living memory. As Arata Isozaki recalled: 'I believe the memory and experience of the great flood that visited Florence had a profound effect on the members of Superstudio and Archizoom who graduated from the University that year. During the flood, the centre of Florence, a symbol of urban culture since the Renaissance, was submerged . . . . Just as the flood was symbolic of the destruction that could level physical culture in an instant, the "Continuous Monument" and the "No-Stop City" are architectural concepts that might launch a destructive attack against the city; at the same time, both are endless objects that might plot a homogeneous, untamed, reckless invasion. . . . Indeed, both projects may well be regarded as metaphors of the flood.'[14]

Zanotta, founded in the 1950s by Aurelia Zanotta, manufactured some of the most avant-garde design of the 1960s, including the 1967 Blow chair by Donato D'Urbino, Paolo Lomazzi and Jonathan De Pas, who had established their Milanese design company the previous year. The inflatable Blow chair is an icon of the 1960s 'throwaway' culture and employed newly developed high-frequency welding techniques for PVC (polyvinyl chloride). It was intended for indoor or outdoor use and was even marketed as suitable for use in swimming-pools, while the chair's transparency was another rebellion against the

traditional association of furniture with permanence. The Blow chair was a 'first' that spurned many imitations, including several French variations in PVC by Nguyen Manh Khan'h (known as Quasar Khan; b. 1934) on which Pop art-inspired decoration was applied. Like paper, PVC was ultimately a Pop material as it was cheap and expendable.

In 1969, Piero Gatti (b. 1940), Cesare Paolini (1937–83) and Franco Teodoro (b. 1939) designed the Sacco, which, like the Blow chair, belonged to a completely new category of furniture. Manufactured by Zanotta, the Sacco was the first beanbag and over the following decades was to prove itself a highly popular and influential design. The Sacco's flexibility was achieved through a filling of polystyrene pellets; its amorphousness allowed it to be moved easily and meant that it was very much in tune with the casual lifestyle of the 1960s.

The French designers Pierre Paulin and Olivier Mourgue created highly sculptural yet essentially rational furniture. Paulin's boldly formed Ribbon chair of 1965 is an inviting and ergonomically superb design. His designs for seat furniture gave great consideration to the user's freedom of movement, an idea that Eero Saarinen had promoted in the late 1940s with his Womb chair. The 577 chair, designed by Paulin in 1967, possesses an effortless visual simplicity and like the Sacco, rests directly on the floor, allowing the user to assume a relaxed and informal posture.

Olivier Mourgue, like Paulin, created novel furniture with elegant and undulating shapes. His Djinn series designed in 1963 was also constructed of tubular steel frames with polyurethane foam upholstery covered in stretch jersey fabric. The expressive plasticity of its forms and the use of boldly coloured textiles gave this furniture a futuristic appearance, so much so that it was used in Stanley Kubrick's film *2001: A Space Odyssey*. One of Mourgue's favourite designs, the 1968 Bouloum lounge chair, is an unusual 'person seat' constructed of foam-upholstered tubular steel. Mourgue wrote: 'Creation is

Eero Aarnio
Pastille or Gyro chair, 1968

sometimes a cry, a reaction against something. Why go on designing objects that claim to be perfect but are already so numerous?'[15] The Bouloum can be seen as a reaction against traditional design formats; it is a chair with an identity, a personality and a sense of humour.

To a limited extent, Surrealism influenced avant-garde furniture design in the 1960s. American designer Wendell Castle, although primarily known for his highly crafted wooden furniture, experimented with reinforced plastics and between 1969 and 1970 produced the surreal Molar and Castle series of sofa and chairs; the Molar sofa, as its name implies, takes the form of a large back tooth. Like Castle's later designs, it was not produced in large numbers and was, in fact, not intended for mass production.

The Italian company Gufram manufactured on a larger scale other Surrealist-inspired furniture, including I Sassi, which was designed by Piero Gilardi in 1967. This set of polyurethane 'boulders' breaks all traditional design conventions and jeers particularly at the idea of truth to materials, a pivotal theme of modernist doctrine. I Sassi attempts to bridge the gap between art and design through its blatant disregard for function.

Scandinavian designers in the 1960s also researched the possibilities now open to them through the technological advances of the plastics industry. Verner Panton's Stacking chair of 1960 was the first chair to achieve a single-piece continuous construction, which initially utilized rigid polyurethane. This unity of form and materials had been the unrealized goal of Eero Saarinen when he designed the Pedestal Group in 1956–57. Panton's Stacking chair adopts the Modern Movement's cantilever principle in plastic to dramatic effect.

Finnish designer Eero Aarnio (b. 1932) created two of the best-known designs of the decade: the Globe chair of 1965 and the Gyro chair of 1968. The Globe chair is an enormous half sphere that is supported on a squat pedestal base. The interior of this 'ultra-modern' fibreglass chair was foam upholstered with a fabric covering and effected a dark, womb-like retreat. The later Gyro chair or, as it is sometimes known, the Pastille, was also constructed of fibreglass and because of the resilience of its materials was intended for interior and exterior use. Scandinavian design was undoubtedly influenced by Pop, but only in the forms it employed, for the Scandinavians refused to incorporate the disposable ethic that was held by the majority of avant-garde designers in both Italy and Britain and continued to rely on high-quality production.

The popular culture of the economically buoyant 1960s was based on an 'enjoy-it-today-sling-it-tomorrow philosophy',[16] which condoned novelty for novelty's sake. The spirit of optimism that produced a widespread quest for new design solutions prevailed until about 1967, when it was succeeded by a general awareness of the potential ecological effects on the planet should mass consumerism expand unabated. It was realized that the earth's limited resources and environment could not sustain unlimited industrial growth. This shift in conscience brought about a marked change in public taste. Most consumers came to prefer craft-based design yet, paradoxically, required greater rationalism. These altered attitudes did not manifest themselves fully in design until after 1972 when the oil crisis and the subsequent world recession dramatically reduced furniture production. The anti-design theories explored by Archizoom and Superstudio, which had evolved from popular culture, were later advanced by Studio Alchymia and Memphis. This progression of anti-design in the late 1970s and early 1980s would culminate in an internationally established style: post-modernism.

62 **Poul Volther**
Corona (EJ 605), 1961

63 **Cesare Leonardi and Franca Stagi**
CL9 Ribbon chair, 1961

64 **Pierre Paulin**
545 armchair, 1963

65 **Vico Magistretti**
    Gaudi chair, 1961

66 **Gerrit Rietveld**
    Steltman Stael, 1963

67 **Peter Murdoch**
    Child's chair, 1963

68 **Yrjo Kukkapuro**
Karuselli chair, 1965

69 **Warren Platner**
Table, 1966

70 (left to right)
Eero Aarnio
Ball or Globe chair, 1965

Joe Colombo
Elda chairs, 1965

Lella and Massimo Vignelli
Saratoga chair, 1964

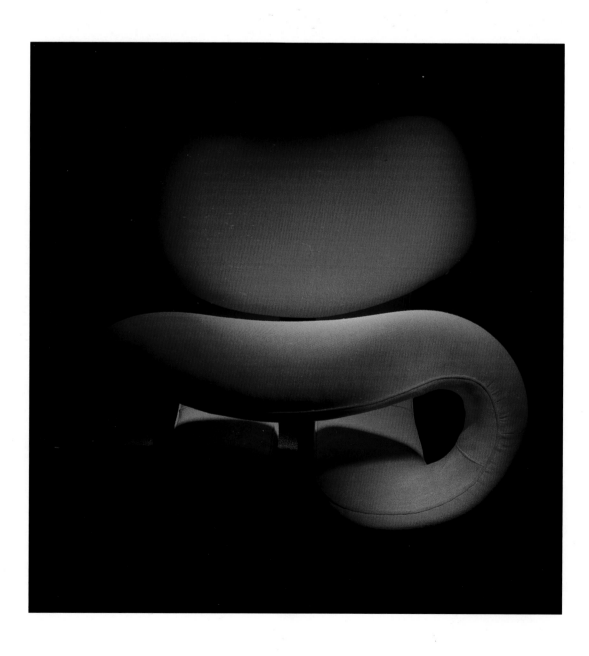

71 **Verner Panton**
Ribbon chair, *c.* 1965

72 **Pierre Paulin**
582 Ribbon chair, 1966

Vico Magistretti
Chimera floor lamp, 1969

73 **Archizoom Associati**
Superonda, 1966

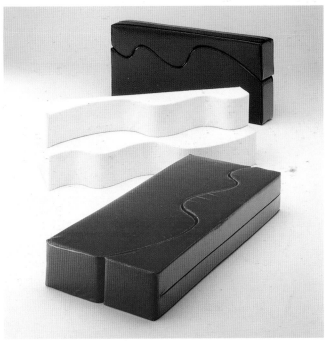

74 **Joe Colombo**
    4867 chair, 1965

75 **Piero Gatti, Cesare Paolini and
    Franco Teodoro**
    Sacco, 1969

76 **Robin Day**
    Polypropylene chair, 1967

77 **Warren Platner**
Warren Platner Collection, 1966

78 **Warren Platner**
Armchair with ottoman, 1966

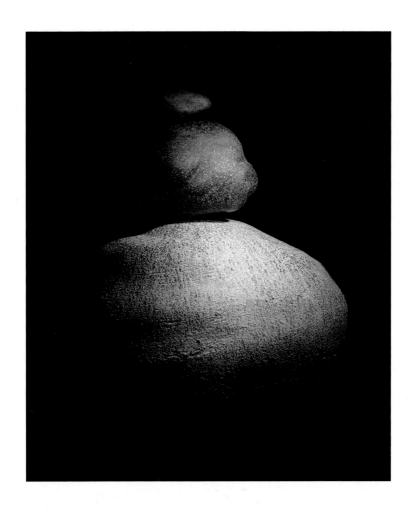

79 **Piero Gilardi**
I Sassi, 1967

80 **Gaetano Pesce**
Up 5 (Donna), 1969

81 **Gaetano Pesce**
Up Series, 1969

82 **Archizoom Associati**
Safari, 1968

83 **Olivier Mourgue**
Bouloum chairs, 1968

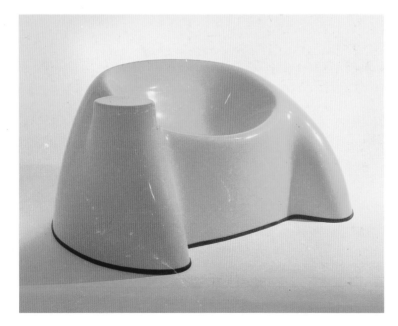

84 **Robin Day**
4-4000 armchair, 1970

85 **Wendell Castle**
Castle chair, 1969–70

Notes on the furniture

Poul Volther, Danish

Corona (EJ 605), 1961 (62)
Erik Jorgensen Mobelfabrik, Denmark

Chromium-plated steel frame supporting
fabric- or leather-covered neoprene-
upholstered plywood seat and back
elements

62

The highly sculptural form of the Corona
chair is reminiscent of Alexander Calder's
mobiles: its four gently curving elliptical
seat elements, graduated in size, appear to
hover in space. The extremely comfortable
Corona is a fine example of high-quality
Scandinavian design and has only recently
been taken out of production.

Cesare Leonardi, Italian, b. 1935 and
Franca Stagi, Italian, b. 1937

CL9 Ribbon chair, 1961 (63)
Elco, Italy

Chromium-plated, bent tubular steel base
supporting moulded and enamelled, glass-
reinforced polyester (GRP) seat section

63

Cesare Leonardi and Franca Stagi opened
their own design office based in Moderna,
Italy in 1961. The large CL9 Ribbon chair
from the same year, like their later Dondolo
rocking chair of 1967, has a fluid sculptural
shape. The CL9's seat and back are formed
from a continuous band of moulded GRP,
which is supported on a cantilevered
tubular steel base. Connected to the seat
with foam-rubber bumpers, the base
assembly allows the chair a moderate
degree of flexibility. The CL9 was initially
manufactured by Bernini, Italy and later in
1969 production was taken over by Elco,
Italy. The CL9 Ribbon chair is no longer in
production.

Pierre Paulin, French, b. 1927

545 armchair, 1963 (64)
Artifort, The Netherlands

Vinyl-, fabric- or leather-covered, latex
foam-upholstered moulded plywood seat
and back elements supported on a brass- or
chromium-plated, four-point pedestal base

With its large and inviting proportions, the
545 armchair is ergonomically highly
refined, a hallmark of all of Pierre Paulin's
seat furniture. This armchair with three
upholstered seat sections and a smaller,
similarly constructed chair with two
sections, the 549 designed in 1961, predicted
the flowing sculptural forms he was to
employ and become renowned for in the
late 1960s. Since the 1950s Paulin has
worked as a design consultant for Artifort
and has also undertaken research for
Mobilier National, Paris. The 545 armchair
was manufactured between 1963 and 1969.

65

64

Vico Magistretti, Italian, b. 1920

Gaudi chair, 1961*(65)
Artemide, Italy

Injection-moulded ABS (Acrylonitrile
Butadiene Styrene)

Magistretti's Gaudi chair, with its sensuous
and subtle form, is a tribute to the
Catalonian architect and designer of the
same name. Designed in about 1961, the
Gaudi chair, like the Selene chair, was
initially constructed of GRP, but it was not
until around 1967 that it was put into mass
production by Artemide, who injection-
moulded it in ABS, a stronger and lighter
plastic. It was originally offered only in
apple-green but was later produced in
several bright colours. Magistretti also
designed a larger version of the Gaudi
known as the Vicario chair. His
sophisticated designs helped to alter the
status of plastic by associating it with
quality and luxury.

Gerrit Rietveld, Dutch, 1888–1964

Steltman Stael, 1963 (66)
G. van der Groenekan, The Netherlands

66

68

Untreated solid oak construction

In the Spring of 1963, work commenced on
a commission that Gerrit Rietveld had
received to refurbish the Steltman Jewelry
Shop, Nordeinde, The Hague. The project,
which included four separate furniture
designs, was completed shortly before
Rietveld's death in June 1964. Two of the
original Steltman chairs designed for the
shop had upholstered seats and were
manufactured by G. van der Groenekan, as
were several other prototypes. With its
block-like construction of solid geometric
forms, the Steltman Stael possesses an
inherent monumentality. After Rietveld's
death a further six Steltman chairs were
produced by the van der Groenekan
workshop and were constructed of solid
elm with either limed or lacquered finishes.

Peter Murdoch, British, b. 1940

Child's chair, 1963 (67)
International Paper, USA

67

Polyethylene-coated, laminated paperboard

Peter Murdoch designed his Child's chair
while studying at the Royal College of Art,
London. One of the first examples of a
mass-produced paper furniture product, the
Child's chair – with its polka-dot motif
inspired by contemporary Op Art, its low
cost and built-in obsolescence – ideally met
the demands of the 1960s mass consumer
market. Using three types of paper to make
up a five-layer lamination, the Child's chair
was surprisingly resilient and perfectly
suited for high-volume manufacture, as one
chair could be produced per second by a
single machine. In their unassembled state,
eight hundred of these chairs could be
stacked into a pile four feet high, allowing
for easy transportation. Sold in flat-pack
form, they were assembled origami fashion
and were produced from 1964 to 1965.

Yrjo Kukkapuro, Finnish, b. 1933

Karuselli chair, 1965 (68)
Haimi Oy, Finland

Steel-reinforced glass-fibre base with
swivelling and rocking chromium-plated
steel cradle, supporting a steel-reinforced
moulded glass-fibre shell with foam-backed
leather upholstery

Yrjo Kukkapuro trained at Helsinki
University before opening his own design
office in 1959. His best-known design, the
412 Karuselli chair, was first exhibited in
1965 at the International Trade Fair,
Helsinki and a year later won the Lunning
Prize. The Karuselli's seat shell was
contoured in such a way as to require only a
thin layer of foam padding: the leather-
covered upholstery was attached with press
studs to facilitate easy removal. The chair's
unusual rocking and swivelling mechanism
allowed the sitter to alter position with a
minimum of effort. The Karuselli chair was
manufactured under licence by Ryman
Conran in Britain, but is no longer in
production.

Warren Platner, American, b. 1919

Table, 1966* (69)
Knoll International, USA

Nickel-plated, electrically welded bent steel
rod base supporting plate-glass top

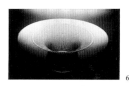

69

Warren Platner worked in the architectural
offices of Raymond Loewy, I.M. Pei and
later Eero Saarinen before establishing his
own practice in 1965. With regard to his
collection of tables and chairs designed for
Knoll International, Platner said, 'As a
designer, I felt that there was room for the
kind of decorative, gentle, graceful kind of
design that appeared in a period style like
Louis XV. But it could have a more rational
base instead of being applied decoration'
(see Eric Larrabee and Massimo Vignelli,

Knoll Design, New York 1981, page 157). The Platner collection possesses a timeless elegance and sophistication which, although inspired in spirit by period styles, is highly innovative in its use of materials. Currently in production, the table is available with a glass or marble top.

70

Interior: Stendig, USA

Eero Aarnio, Finnish, b. 1932

Ball or **Globe chair**, 1965 (70)
Asko Oy, Finland

Fabric-covered, latex foam-upholstered, glass-fibre shell supported on circular metal pedestal base

Eero Aarnio established his own design office in 1962 and has worked as an industrial and interior designer, specializing in furniture design that utilizes synthetic materials, believing that designers should make use of state-of-the-art technology wherever possible. The innovative Globe chair resulted from Aarnio's conscious distancing of his work from traditional chair forms and was a successful attempt at expressing the iconoclasm of the 1960s. While the Globe chair was first designed in 1963, the example illustrated was produced in 1965. The Globe functioned as a micro-environment by totally enveloping the sitter and was available in a variety of colours. It is no longer in production.

Joe Colombo, Italian, 1930–71

Elda chairs, 1965 (70)
Comfort, Italy

Self-supporting, moulded-fibreglass shell with an integrated rotating drum base, the seat interior upholstered with leather or fabric covering and seven foam-filled cushions

Joe Colombo, unlike most other Italian architect-designers, developed his furniture designs on paper, through drawings and blueprints, rather than with models. He was an accomplished draughtsman who had originally worked as a painter, sculptor and illustrator in the 1950s. The futuristic and exceptionally comfortable Elda chair of 1963 was the first large armchair produced

in fibreglass and won an A.I.D. International Design Award in 1968; the chair illustrated was produced in 1965. It is no longer in production.

Lella Vignelli, Italian and **Massimo Vignelli**, Italian b. 1931

Saratoga chair, 1964 (70)
Poltronova, Italy

Enamelled wood construction with fabric-covered, foam-upholstered seat

The geometric simplicity of the Saratoga chair alludes to the Vignellis' graphic work based on Euclidian geometry and grid systems. The Vignellis founded their own design office in 1960 and since then have designed furniture, glassware, silverware, interiors and exhibitions, as well as the graphics for which they are best known. They write: 'We believe in improving the visual quality of our environment and in the commitment to achieve this goal; in design dignity and its influence on people; and in timelessness and change, in consistency and contradiction, and in classicism and friendliness. We love to affect design and affect others by design. We love to create and to transform until projects, objects, and ideas become things' (*see* Ann Lee Morgan, *Contemporary Designers*, London 1985, page 610). The Saratoga chair is no longer in production.

Verner Panton, Danish, b. 1926

Ribbon chair, *c.* 1965 (71)
Manufacturer unknown

71

Jersey-covered, latex foam-upholstered bent tubular steel frame

Verner Panton exploited the potential of new materials in the creation of striking and often highly sculptural designs. His curvilinear Ribbon chair uses foam rubber wrapped over a steel frame to achieve its elegant, continuous form. Like Pierre Paulin and Olivier Mourgue, Panton took full advantage of the expressive possibilities that this relatively simple type of construction offered. He also designed in the mid-1960s a 'Living Tower', which was a monumental structure incorporating four seating levels. These quintessentially avant-garde Pop designs can be seen as experiments in the search for new seating formats. The Ribbon chair and the Living Tower are no longer in production.

Pierre Paulin, French, b. 1927

582 Ribbon chair, 1966* (72)
Artifort, The Netherlands

Tensioned rubber sheet over a bent, tubular metal frame with jersey-covered, latex-foam upholstery supported on a lacquered wood base

The 582 Ribbon chair was first shown as a prototype at the Utrecht Furniture Exhibition, 1965 and was further developed for production in 1966. Paulin's most sculptural chair design, it is also his most comfortable, with its generously proportioned wrap-around seat area, which allows the sitter to adopt a number of relaxed positions. In fitting tribute to Paulin's genius for creating novel seating solutions, the Ribbon chair won an A.I.D. International Design Award in 1969 and is still in production, with a matching ottoman P582.

72

Vico Magistretti, Italian, b. 1920

Chimera floor lamp, 1969* (72)
Artemide, Italy

Moulded opaque perspex shade on enamelled metal base

Vico Magistretti's Chimera lamp is one of his most celebrated designs for lighting and is available in two versions, floor and table height (Mezza). The construction accommodates three fluorescent bulbs; the light is subtly diffused along the lamp's continuous moulded shade. Supremely elegant, both versions of the Chimera lamp are currently in production.

Archizoom Associati, Italian, 1966–74

Superonda, 1966* (73)
Poltronova, Italy

Vinyl-covered polyurethane foam construction

Cut from a single block of polyurethane foam, the Superonda (Superwave) was simple and inexpensive to produce, requiring no expensive tooling. Its two separate sections, when laid end to end, create a continuous wave-like form. It can be used as a sofa, as illustrated, or turned through 90 degrees and used as a chaise-longue. Not particularly functional, the Superonda is more of a plaything than a serious design solution. It is, however, still in production and is available in white, black and red glossy vinyl.

73

74

Joe Colombo, Italian, 1930–71

4867 chair, 1965* (74)
Kartell, Italy

Injection-moulded 'Durethan' nylon

The 4867, Seggio or Universale stacking chair designed in 1965 was originally intended for an aluminium construction. When it was put into production in 1967, however, the materials were changed to plastic – 'Cycolac' ABS – and it was the first chair to be entirely injection moulded. The materials were changed again in 1971 to 'Durethan' nylon, which had been developed by the Bayer company: a material so resilient that Kartell gave the chair a five-year guarantee when purchased. The 4867 had interchangeable legs of two heights and could be stacked into sets of three. The chair is illustrated with the 4310 table designed in 1984 by Anna Ferrieri-Castelli. Both designs are currently produced by Kartell, a company which was founded in 1949 to explore the potential of plastics in the production of consumer products.

Piero Gatti, Italian, b. 1940, **Cesare Paolini**, Italian, 1937–83 and **Franco Teodoro**, Italian, b. 1939

Sacco, 1969* (75)
Zanotta, Italy

Leather or vinyl bag filled with semi-expanded polystyrene beads

The Sacco was a revolutionary seating concept which spawned many imitations. Essentially a bean-bag, its cover was constructed of either PVC or leather and it was filled with approximately twelve million semi-expanded polystyrene beads, each 3mm in diameter. The Sacco adapted its shape to suit any sitter and was therefore very much in tune with the informal lifestyle of the 1960s.

76 75

Robin Day, British, b. 1915

Polypropylene chair, 1967* (76)
Hille International & Co. Ltd, UK

Injection-moulded polypropylene seat shell supported on tubular metal legs

The Polypropylene armchair was a version of the Polypropylene side chair which Robin Day designed in 1963. Polypropylene had been invented by the Italian Nobel Peace Prize winner, Professor Giulio Natta in 1954 and was subsequently produced by Montecatini and later Shell. It was perfectly suited to furniture production, for it was both lighter than GRP and less expensive. For the first time in furniture design history, truly low-cost, high-quality seat furniture could be mass produced. The Polypropylene side chairs were the first designs to exploit the full potential of this new and remarkable plastic and the injection-moulding process. The chairs were designed so that various metal bases could be attached to the seat shells, allowing for multi-purpose applications. Although tooling up was expensive, when in place a single tool could produce four thousand chairs a week. Both designs are still in production and are available in a variety of colours.

Warren Platner, American, b. 1919

Warren Platner Collection, 1966* (77)
Knoll International, USA

Nickel-plated, electrically welded, bent steel rod constructions, the tables with glass or marble tops, the chairs and stools with foam-filled cushions, the lounge and easy chair with fabric-covered, foam-upholstered, moulded fibreglass shells

77

The elegant Platner Collection, manufactured by Knoll International from 1966 to the present, has helped Warren Platner win international recognition as a furniture designer. Platner reveals that, as a designer, 'You hope to produce a classic. A classic is something that every time you look at it, you accept it as it is and you can see no way of improving it. You can refine forever, but you reach a point where you're moving backwards. I think Emerson said something like, "Really strong things have a certain amount of awkwardness about them; otherwise they become weak." I have never designed anything that I wanted to change to improve it. When I finished it I turned myself off, or I would have over-refined it, and it would no longer have had any strength' (*see* Eric Larrabee and Massimo Vignelli, *Knoll Design*, New York 1981, page 157).

Warren Platner, American, b. 1919

Armchair with ottoman, 1966* (78)
Knoll International, USA

Nickel-plated, electrically welded bent steel rod construction supporting a fabric-covered, foam-upholstered moulded fibreglass shell, the ottoman and chair with foam-filled cushions

78

In their complex construction, the wire bases of Platner's armchair (or Easy chair) and ottoman exploit the optical effects created by light and shadow, thereby echoing contemporary developments in Op Art. Like Bertoia's earlier series of bent rod chairs, the Platner Collection can be seen as a study of space and form. The chairs and ottoman are available in a range of coloured textiles.

Piero Gilardi, Italian, b. 1900

I Sassi, 1967* (79)
Gufram, Italy

Moulded 'Guflex' polyurethane foam with
'Guflac' lacquered finish

Like other furniture produced by Gufram, I
Sassi (Rocks) and the larger Sedil-Sasso
(Stone Seat) are highly surreal in content.
Although it has the appearance of solid
rock, I Sassi is surprisingly soft. Once the
moulding process is completed, I Sassi is
realistically painted and applied with a
lacquer coating, which is both weather-
resistent and waterproof. Both I Sassi and
Sedil-Sasso are in production.

79

80

Gaetano Pesce, Italian, b. 1939

Up 5 (Donna), 1969 (80)
B & B Italia, Italy

Moulded polyurethane foam covered in
stretch nylon jersey

The chairs that formed part of Pesce's Up
Series, when boxed, were compressed to a
tenth of their original size and vacuum-
packed into a PVC wrapping. When the
plastic envelope was opened the Up chairs
literally bounced into life, returning to their
full volume; transforming the purchase of
furniture into a 'happening'. Up 5 was
intended to represent a woman: 'The shape
of the armchair has anatomic
characteristics and makes some undeniably
anthropomorphic references. It is, indeed
like a huge maternal lap which reminds one
of the prehistoric votive statuettes of
fertility' (*see* Mario Mastropietro, *An
Industry for Design: The Research,
Designers & Corporate Image of B & B
Italia*, Milan 1982, page 246). The Up Series
is no longer in production.

Gaetano Pesce, Italian, b. 1939

Up Series, 1969 (81)
B & B Italia, Italy

81

Moulded polyurethane foam covered in
stretch nylon jersey

The Up Series consisted of seven designs:
Up 1 to Up 6 were pieces of
'transformation' furniture while Up 7 (not
illustrated) was formed as a giant foot. The
series (excluding Up 7, which was flesh-
coloured) was offered in three types of
stretch jersey and ten colours and was
packaged in flat boxes designed by Enrico
Trabacchi, so could be purchased 'off the
shelf'. When first shown, the Up Series
captured the attention of the world press,
creating for Pesce an international
reputation as a highly innovative and
individual designer, a status that he still
maintains.

Archizoom Associati, Italian, 1966–74

Safari, 1968 (82)
Poltronova, Italy

Glass fibre-reinforced polyester frame with
fabric-covered foam upholstery

82

This sectional 'livingscape' confronts the
viewer with its monumental immobility.
Covered in imitation leopard skin, the
Safari alludes to kitsch design from the
1950s. It was intended as a statement of
opposition to the Modern Movement's
tenets of 'good design' and therefore 'good
taste'. The format of the Safari was inspired
more by architecture than by traditional
forms of seating.

Olivier Mourgue, French, b. 1939

Bouloum chairs, 1968* (83)
Arconas, Canada

Indoor version with fabric-covered, foam-
upholstered bent tubular steel frame,
outdoor version with gel-coated, moulded
fibreglass shell

83

An anthropomorphous chaise-longue or 'person-seat', the Bouloum was named after a childhood friend of the designer. Mourgue travelled with, wrote anecdotes about and photographed Bouloum in various situations. His intention was to create a piece of furniture with a personality: a novel idea and an interesting alternative to the modernist 'machine-for-sitting' concept. Bouloum is currently in production and offered in a range of 29 colours; a Bouloum room divider is also available.

Robin Day, British, b. 1915

4–4000 armchair, 1970 (84)
Hille International & Co. Ltd, UK

Enamelled metal pedestal base supporting an injection-moulded ABS seat shell with fabric-covered and buttoned foam upholstery

84

The large 4–4000 armchair formed part of Robin Day's Living Scene range of furniture, which was intended for a younger market than the traditional Hille clientele. The injection-moulded shell of the chair was strong enough to require no reinforcing and it was inexpensive to manufacture. The 4–4000 and the other Living Scene furniture is no longer in production.

Wendell Castle, American, b. 1932

Castle chair, 1969–70 (85)
Beylerian Limited, USA for Wendell Castle Associates, USA

Moulded, glass-reinforced polyester (GRP)

85

Wendell Castle is primarily known for his virtuoso work in wood, but in the late 1960s he produced two series of designs, the Castle group and the Molar group, which were constructed of moulded GRP. He found that the fluid organic forms central to his handcrafted work translated well into plastic; he created 'more personal and unique sculptural form(s) than usual in fibreglass or reinforced plastic' (*see* D. Taragin, E. S. Cooke and J. Giovanni, *Furniture by Wendell Castle*, New York 1989, page 42). He believed that his designs in synthetic materials qualified both as sculpture and as functional furniture. Both the Castle and Molar groups were produced in limited numbers and were retailed exclusively by Stendig; they are no longer in production.

111

1970 to 1980   Conformist, reformist or contesting

Fred Scott
Elephant chair, 1972

**Jonathan De Pas, Donato
D'Urbino** and **Paolo Lomazzi**
Sciangai clothes stand, 1973

Shiro Kuramata
Drawers in irregular form, 1977

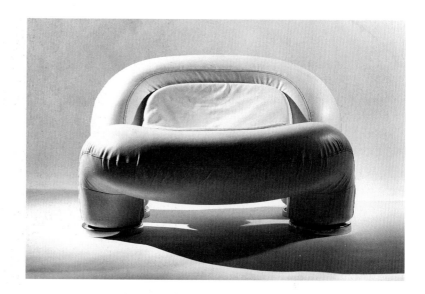

4

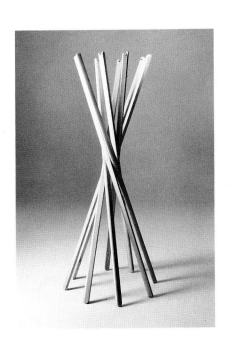

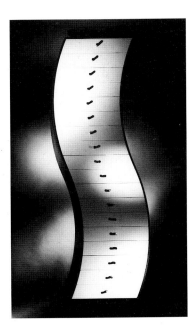

The spirit of Pop culture continued to manifest itself in furniture design until about 1972. With the general energy crisis of 1973, petroleum by-products such as plastics dramatically increased in price and were no longer seen as viable materials for the production of inexpensive, expendable furniture. Rationalism and anti-design became more polarized than ever, as the mood shifted in the mass market towards a conservative and socially responsible approach to design. The influence of Pop was gradually replaced by economic and environmental concerns. Worldwide recession in 1975 compelled manufacturers, now severely limited by cost constraints, to incorporate rigorously rational methods of production in order to remain competitive. From this date, mainstream designers distanced themselves from the exuberance and excess of the 1960s and created anonymous, rationally designed furniture for both the domestic and contract markets.

During this period of economic uncertainty, Italy persevered and resolutely employed design as an essential tool in maintaining its export levels. Radical design continued to be promoted by a minority of mainly avant-garde designers, but by the mid-1970s, the division between rational and anti-rational design was becoming less clear-cut, for there was a growing debate over its definition, centring on whether or not a design could be considered radical if it was realizable. Designers such as Gaetano Pesce and design groups like Studio 65 and Gruppo Strum believed that it was possible to actualize radical design. Although this furniture was intended for a narrow sector of the market, it was produced in limited numbers by those major manufacturers who felt it necessary to stay in touch with the avant-garde. While this progressive furniture was well received by the press, other designers preferred to pursue radical design theoretically, from a political and intellectual perspective. In the late 1970s and early 1980s, radical design became more articulate, élitist and self-conscious and as a result, its popular appeal dissipated.

The difficult economic conditions throughout the 1970s necessitated the dominance of rationalism in the furniture industry. As a result, nearly all vestiges of ornament and symbolism were eradicated by cost-conscious manufacturers, who obligated designers to work within highly restrictive briefs. A stylistic spin-off of this overwhelming return to rationalist principles was High-Tech. Named after a book written by Joan Kron and Suzanne Slesin in 1978, High-Tech design expressed a continuing confidence in the future and a faith in the social potency of advanced technology. Although primarily a domestic style, it was based on industrial systems of production and utilized materials that were generally associated with heavy industry, such as steel scaffolding, stamped metal and rubber flooring. High-Tech furniture imitated rationally designed industrial equipment and was often retailed in an unassembled state so that it could be purchased off the shelf. This approach kept its cost generally low and thereby contributed to its popular appeal, especially among the growing numbers of younger consumers.

The Omkstak chair, designed in 1971 by Central School of Art graduate Rodney Kinsman, is one of the most elegant examples of High-Tech design. Kinsman realized that if he was to enter the furniture market successfully in this time of economic uncertainty, he would have to produce low-cost, multi-purpose products. He therefore ensured that his consultancy, OMK (run in collaboration with Jurek Olejnik and Bryan Morrison), employed inexpensive methods of production. The Omkstak incorporates stamped steel, so, in its use of materials, can be seen as a modern reworking of Hans Coray's Landi chair of 1938. Available in a variety of coloured paint finishes and intended for both interior and exterior use, the Omkstak is supremely functional, can be stacked and clipped into rows, and like the Landi chair, possesses an enduring aesthetic. Kinsman remarks: 'It is irresponsible to design things that

don't last visually. I don't believe that products should have such an ephemeral form that they will be out of date long before they should be. We all live by fashions, but with furniture, you can't just rely on colour or some formal gimmick, there has to be something deeper.'[1]

In the rapidly expanding contract market, commercial specifiers insisted on integrated office systems that could provide a high degree of flexibility within the working environment. Through the introduction of furniture such as Herman Miller's enormously influential Action Office System of 1968, the gap between the contract and domestic markets had already been substantially widened. It is therefore ironic that one of the most successful pieces of contract furniture was the individual Supporto chair. Designed in 1979 by Fred Scott (b. 1942) and manufactured by Hille, the Supporto has an upholstered, cast-aluminium construction with a gas cylinder mechanism for raising and lowering the seat. Like many other contract chairs, its production includes a range of variations, but the widespread popularity of the Supporto itself is due to the chair's form, which derives almost exclusively from ergonomic considerations.

Scandinavian designers in the 1970s responded to the new ecological awareness with a style that employed as few materials as possible. Inspired by the arguments put forward in *Nomadic Furniture* by American critic Victor Papanek, Swedish designers such as Johan Huldt (b. 1942) and Jan Dranger designed a range of furniture composed solely of tubular steel frames with slip-on canvas covers. A similar movement arose in Finland, where the plastic furniture of Eero Aarnio from the previous decade was now considered both ecologically and financially unsound. The chair designs of Yrjo Kukkapuro (b. 1933), for example, helped to bring about a revival of Finnish furniture design, which again was founded on the use of materials from an easily renewable resource, such as wood and leather, simple tooling, and minimal use of expensive technological processes.

Against the predominance of both rationalism and spare, ecologically sound design, many avant-garde furniture designers continued to explore the potential of anti-design. The concerns of this movement in the 1970s, however, were political and social, unlike the generally commercial aims of anti-design during the 1960s. One of the last – and most significant – truly Pop-inspired series of designs was created by Canadian-born architect Frank Gehry (b. 1929) in 1972. His Easy Edges Group consisted of seventeen pieces of furniture, each constructed of laminated, corrugated cardboard, and was intended for the mass market. Like Peter Murdoch's earlier production of the Child's chair and Those Things collection, Easy Edges utilized simple technology and inexpensive paper products in an imaginative way. Gehry's transformation of a material traditionally associated with utilitarian packaging into strong and resilient, subtly designed, low-cost furniture, is a demonstration of his unquestionable talent.

The Easy Edges Group was initially manufactured by Jack Brogan and was briefly reissued by Chiru in 1982. It was retailed through prominent department stores such as Bloomingdales in New York; although it achieved immediate success, Gehry, who held the patent on Easy Edges, withdrew the line after only three months. He was concerned that his ascendancy as a popular furniture designer would distract him from realizing his potential as an architect. Having recommitted himself to his original profession, Gehry later became a pre-eminent American architect. He did, however, return to furniture design in the early 1980s, when he created the anti-commercial, anti-functional Experimental Edges, which were also constructed of corrugated cardboard. Unlike Easy Edges, however, these limited-edition pieces, with rough, unfinished surfaces, were conceived of as art furniture and were retailed exclusively through specialist art galleries.

Although Italian anti-design of the early 1970s ran counter to the mass-market objectives of Pop, it was still

influenced by Pop-art imagery. Claes Oldenburg's sculptures inspired over-sized and out-of-context pieces of furniture such as the Joe chair, designed by Jonathan De Pas, Donato D'Urbino and Paolo Lomazzi in 1970. Manufactured by Poltronova, this giant baseball glove, constructed of leather-upholstered polyurethane foam, was named after the New York Yankee baseball player, Joe DiMaggio. The materials used made it extremely expensive to retail and it was believed by many critics to be a costly and, perhaps, inane joke. In fact, it may well have been a wry comment on the proliferation of reissued Bauhaus furniture, which was upholstered in high-priced glove leather.

The Italian manufacturer Gufram produced some of the most interesting anti-design furniture of the early 1970s, furniture created in the same spirit as the company's I Sassi rocks of the previous decade. Capitello, a moulded-foam chair in the shape of a large Ionic capital, was designed by Studio 65 in 1971 and predicted the work of post-modern classicists such as Robert Venturi (b. 1925) and Hans Hollein (b. 1934). Studio 65 also produced a reworking of Salvador Dali's 1936 Mae West sofa, which was renamed the Marilyn sofa, after the actress Marilyn Monroe, and covered in a bright-red stretch fabric. This polyurethane-foam sofa represents an early example of 'redesign'; a concept that would be explored more fully by Alessandro Mendini in the late 1970s. Another highly surreal design manufactured by Gufram was Il Pratone, or, as it is sometimes known, Big Meadow. Designed by Gruppo Strum in 1971, this giant-sized patch of turf in moulded foam, though surprisingly soft to sit on, had little practical application as a piece of furniture. Although these 'reformist' designs attracted a significant amount of publicity in design journals, they had no direct influence on the mass furniture market.

Two important exhibitions in this period reviewed the work of Italian radical designers. The show entitled 'Design als Postulat: am Beispiel Italien' took place at the IDZ in Berlin,

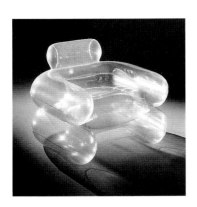

Jonathan De Pas, Donato D'Urbino and Paolo Lomazzi
Blow chair, 1967

while in New York in 1972, in recognition of the continuing influence of innovative Italian furniture design, the Museum of Modern Art staged the exhibition 'Italy: New Domestic Landscape – Achievements and Problems of Italian Design'. Because of the economic recession that Italy was already experiencing, the New York exhibition turned out to be a retrospective, which celebrated the evolution of design in Italy from the 1960s. The retrospective mood of this period in Italian design was also expressed in a number of influential publications, which further eroded the optimism of previous years. Architect and designer Emilio Ambasz, the organizer of the exhibition, identified in the accompanying catalogue three directions in Italian design: conformist, reformist and contesting. 'Conformist' work maintained the modernist tradition of rationalism and included furniture by Vico Magistretti, Marco Zanuso and Richard Sapper. 'Reformist' work, although inspired by radical design, was created within the constraints of manufacturing technology and the marketplace; avant-garde design that could be realized. This category comprised furniture by, among others, Joe Colombo, Ettore Sottsass and Gae Aulenti. 'Contesting' designers accused their 'reformist' counterparts of having betrayed their political ideals by allowing their designs to be produced on a commercial basis; truly radical or 'contesting' design was explored by Gaetano Pesce and by groups such as Superstudio, Archizoom, Gruppo Strum and 9999 through conceptual installations which projected utopian, alternative approaches to design.

Although the majority of the 'New Domestic Landscape' exhibits were individual pieces already in production, several prominent designers and design groups were specially commissioned to produce domestic micro-environments and transportable living spaces. Presented with this unique opportunity, both 'conformist' and 'reformist' designers dislayed compact, flexible units that represented an attempt to provide tangible solutions to existing design problems. In opposition

to this practical approach, the new wave designers endeavoured to alter radically the status quo of design through the presentation of experimental concepts which emphasized ideology, politics and sociology. An example of this 'contesting' design was Archizoom's project entitled Empty Room: an installation consisting of a totally void, grey-painted room, in which was played a recorded audio loop of a small girl describing a brightly lit and highly coloured interior. Archizoom's intention was to point out that architecture did not necessarily have to be a 'machine for living', but could inspire society to disassociate itself from a constrictive culture and consumer-driven economic systems.

Radical designers and groups like Archizoom believed that the creativity inherent in society was bounded by the cultural conditioning of social, moral, religious and aesthetic values. Their primary goal was the creation of a 'culture-less' society, which would allow a greater freedom of expression and the discovery of limitless creative talent. Andrea Branzi writes: 'The reduction of reality to solely quantitative parameters was the direction in which the avant-garde was moving . . . we wished to change the social use of culture itself . . . the regaining of all one's own creative faculties as a natural right was for us the new social use of culture; the production of models of behaviour by culture is a feature of the organization of production in society. Hence to deny culture meant to reject work. We realize that all culture is repressive: the functional separation between the producers and the consumers of culture. If all men are equal, only an improper distinction exists between consumer and artist, based on the social division of labour. Cultural atrophy, we claimed, was an extremely serious form of alienation, which prevented the production and consumption of one's own creative activity as a manifestation of spontaneous communication.'[2]

The ideology that supposed spontaneous creativity would deliver man from labour is even more utopian

Burkhard Vogtherr
Hombre chairs, 1971

in spirit than the Modern Movement's attempt to lessen the burden of work through advanced industrial systems. The radical movement believed that a consumer-led society could not redress political and social problems. It was argued that in such a society, leisure time had to be used to regain the energy to produce more; leisure time was therefore consumer-based. The radical groups theorized that if this 'free' time was increased, individual members of society would be able to explore their own personal spontaneous creativity which, in the final analysis, would cause the breakdown of cultural organization; replacing mass-production with mass-creativity. The concept of a classless and cultureless society which could be created and enjoyed by the masses, rather than simply by an educated élite, was the central tenet of radical design philosophy.

In this climate of heady aspirations, Global Tools was officially founded in 1974, a 'school' of counter-architecture and design that brought together the main Italian exponents of radical design in the pursuit a unified programme of research. Based in Florence, Global Tools was a loose-knit co-operative of studios and workshops, which held seminars to teach young designers how to use various tools. There was an emphasis on interaction between 'master' and 'student' and it was at one of these workshops that Ettore Sottsass met Marco Zanini (b. 1954), who later became one of the founding members of Memphis. Simple techniques were encouraged and advanced technology was denied in an attempt to develop the individual's inner creativity. With its belief in *arte povera*, Global Tools was seemingly promoting the idea that virtue can be gained through poverty. This placed the school in a paradoxical position, for poverty can be viewed as a social pattern within a consumer society; fundamental to radical design doctrine was the dissolution of all consumer-based systems driven by a market economy. Global Tools was disbanded in 1975, marking the end of the first phase of 1970s anti-design. In 1976, Ugo la Pietra wrote an article

entitled, 'Where has radical architecture gone?' and at a conference in Bologna in 1978, Alessandro Mendini announced the death of the movement.

A hopeful phenomenon that occurred in the middle of the decade was the astonishing growth in the number of small design and manufacturing companies. At a time when the reputation of Italian design was under threat, as a result of compromises necessitated by the recession and concomitant inflation, these small, flexible organizations successfully upheld the high quality of Italian furniture.

Indeed, anti-design also continued to progress after 1975, if now even further removed from commercial production. Alessandro Mendini, editor of *Casabella* from 1970 to 1976, replaced Gio Ponti as editor of *Domus* in 1979. Mendini was one of the founding members of Studio Alchymia, a design group formed by the architect Alessandro Guerriero (b. 1934) in Milan in 1976; Milan was now indisputably the pre-eminent centre of innovative Italian design. Guerriero established Alchymia for 'the projection of new pictorial worlds in the twentieth century'[3] and owned a gallery where he held annual exhibitions of furniture and objects by designers whose work he considered outside the mainstream of rational design.

Studio Alchymia reiterated the anti-design principles of Pop with an intellectual, rather than commercial, objective of demolishing the barriers between the fine and decorative arts and architecture. During this period, performance art gained increasing popularity and the early work produced by Studio Alchymia can be seen as 'performance design', as it intentionally distanced itself from profit-orientated markets. The designs 'projected' by Studio Alchymia were statements rather than functional objects and ran counter to the rationalist precepts for which Italy was now famed worldwide.

The designers aligned to Studio Alchymia considered rationalism excessively dogmatic. Through the

James Butchart
Flight table, *c.* 1972

application of symbolism and decoration, they attempted to breathe back some spontaneity and life into design, which they believed had become stale, sterile and too serious-minded during the mid-1970s. They rejected the conservatism that had crept back into furniture design and determinedly promoted the use of new materials, at a time when traditional forms and materials held more appeal for manufacturers facing financial decline. Any reference to function was abandoned and replaced with quotations from mass culture and past styles.

Studio Alchymia's members included established designers such as Ettore Sottsass, Andrea Branzi, Riccardo Dalisi (b. 1931) and Alessandro Mendini, as well as younger designers, such as Paola Navone (b. 1950) and Michele De Lucchi (b. 1951). Importantly, Studio Alchymia effected the interaction of these two generations of designers, who derived mutual benefit from a free exchange of ideas. It is not surprising that the first two 'collections' exhibited by the group, ironically entitled, Bau Haus 1 and Bau Haus 2, utilized historical fine art imagery and decorative motifs from the 1950s. Indeed, the first major retrospective of Italian 1950s design was organized by Andrea Branzi and Michele De Lucchi in 1977, at Centrokappa, near Milan. Studio Alchymia's preferment of anti-rational, historicizing decoration and forms and 'poor' manufacturing techniques, did have an Italian precedent: Neo-Liberty, a short-lived style that had flourished briefly in the early 1950s. Inspired by the British Arts and Crafts Movement, Neo-Liberty offered a valid alternative to the modernism of the postwar period.

Central to many of Studio Alchymia's furniture designs was a tongue-in-cheek humour, which attempted to strip away the pretensions that had surrounded the 'good forms' of the preceding decades. In 1978, Mendini created his first examples of 'redesign': the Joe Colombo Stacking chair received an applied faux marble finish, while ensigns were attached to a Gio Ponti Superleggera, thereby

making a reference to the fishermen of Chiavari, who for centuries had used a similar type of chair. Andrea Branzi explains: 'Operations of redesign consisted of touching-up found objects or famous products of design to illustrate the impossibility of designing something new in respect to what has already been designed.'[4]

The in-jokes common to 'banal design' attempted to demonstrate that the intellectual content of furniture designs can, in some circumstances, derive solely from ornament. Proust's armchair, redesigned by Mendini in 1978 and his Kandinsky sideboard of the same year, are early examples of banal design. Both were existing pieces of furniture to which Mendini applied painted decoration inspired by the work of French Neo-Impressionist painter Georges Seurat (1859–91), as well as by that of Wassily Kandinsky.

Studio Alchymia's intention was to destroy the traditional presumption that the fine arts are of a higher aesthetic order than the decorative arts. They not only mocked 'high art' but 'good design' as well. This they achieved effectively through their redesigned 'classic' pieces of furniture, such as Mendini's 1983 version of Marcel Breuer's Wassily chair, which was decorated with coloured amorphous shapes, obscuring its pure lines. American architect Charles Jencks wrote that redesign 'improves a mass-produced cliché by adding things to it'.[5] Andrea Branzi expressed the pessimism that underlies this approach when he wrote, in 1984: 'Redesign emerges out of an attempt to demonstrate that from today and for at least ten years into the future, one can do nothing but redesign.'[6]

However plausible it sounded at the time, Branzi's prediction would not come true, even with regard to post-modernism. Studio Alchymia rejected the utopian aspirations of radical design as expressed by design groups such as Superstudio and 9999 and created élitist furniture that was intended to possess material and aesthetic permanence. Alchymia's early designs were prototypical statements and it was not until the mid-1980s that the aligned manufacturer, Atelier

Paola Navone
Bau Haus 1 and Bau Haus 2
chair, 1979–80

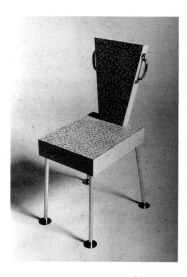

Alchymia, produced its furniture in limited quantities.

Studio Alchymia formulated a language of design where ironic comment and ornamentation were regarded as paramount, while functionalism remained of minimal importance. Through questioning and subsequently rejecting rationalism and consumerism, while embracing decoration, historicism and eclecticism, Studio Alchymia can be seen as the major precursor of post-modernism. Although both Studio Alchymia and the post-modern movement advocated the belief that the principles of modernism were no longer valid, however, their objectives were fundamentally different. The sole intention of Studio Alchymia's use of decorative elaboration was to imply conceptually the end of 'good design'. While accepting the technological advances of modernism, post-modernists promoted the reintroduction and liberation of decoration in design for its own sake, through historical references, and advocated a return to traditional, pre-Modern Movement values.

In the 1970s, Ettore Sottsass was the primary Italian exponent of anti-design, which he promoted through projects such as Mobili Grigi, designed in 1970 for the 'Eurodomus' exhibition in Milan. His work became increasingly influential and, by the early part of the decade, he was regarded by the younger generation of designers as a guru of anti-design. In 1978, Sottsass collaborated with Studio Alchymia and from this date, his furniture designs often comprised simple, block-like shapes in bold colours, with quotations from previous decorative styles. In his later work for Memphis, in the 1980s, he would include zoomorphic forms and decorative motifs inspired by Pop art and would become the principal executant of post-modernism in the decorative arts.

As with the majority of major styles, post-modernism first became apparent in architecture and later revealed itself in the decorative arts. The style originated from the rejection of modernism in the 1960s and although it was not until the late 1970s that it was clearly defined as an important movement in architecture and design, the term 'post-modernism' was first used by Nikolaus Pevsner in his 1968 publication, *Studies in Art, Architecture and Design: Victorian and After*. In 1977 Charles Jencks wrote his highly influential treatise, *The Language of Post-Modern Architecture*, in which he stated: 'Happily we can date the death of modern architecture to a precise moment in time. Modern architecture died in St. Louis, Missouri on the 15th July 1972.'[7] In this statement he makes reference to the demolition of the modernist Pruitt-Igoe skyscrapers, which had been constructed only twenty years earlier. Jencks was a vehement critic of Modern Movement architecture and dubbed the rectilinear, high-rise buildings that characterize so many urban skylines as 'dumb boxes'. The social deficiencies of modernism had been identified and there was an exigency for a new manner of design; a different vocabulary of form. In 1978, Jencks interpreted the emerging style, post-modernism, as 'double coding: the combination of modern techniques with something else in order for architecture (or design) to communicate with the public and a concerned minority, usually other architects'.[8]

Although post-modernism was essentially a phenomenon of the early 1980s, precedents were being set from the mid-1960s through the writings of Robert Venturi, among others, in anticipation of a new mainstream style. Venturi, a Princeton graduate, who had worked in the architectural practice of Eero Saarinen and Louis Kahn, was a pioneer of post-modernism. In his 1966 book entitled, *Complexity and Contradiction in Architecture*, Venturi had called for, 'elements which are hybrid rather than pure ... messy vitality over obvious unity',[9] and had insisted, 'I prefer "both-and" to "either-or" ',[10] in an appeal for variety and choice in architecture and design. Although eclecticism had been a central theme in interior design from the turn of the decade, Venturi was vindicating its use within the design of

John Makepeace
Ebony and Nickel-Silver chair,
1978

individual objects and within single architectural briefs. In 1972, he co-wrote with Denise Scott-Brown (who was later to become his wife) and Steve Izenour, *Learning from Las Vegas*. In this manifesto, Venturi impels architects to include a variety of references in their work, especially quotations drawn from American popular mass culture. It is important to note that he did not support the use of decorative embellishment for its own sake, rather, he insisted that ornamentation have coherence and content. He viewed Las Vegas, for example, as a genuine manifestation of popular fantasy, finding a cultural honesty in its kitsch, neon-lit architecture.

In the late 1970s there was a general trend away from conceptual art towards a new figurative style in painting, which included the work of artists such as Julian Schnabel (b. 1951) and Georg Baselitz (b. 1938). The widespread popularity of this Neo-Expressionism in fine art coincided with the international acceptance of post-modernism and the representational use of decoration in architecture and design. Both of these movements reflected the public's preference for accessible themes with which it could readily identify. By the end of the decade, furniture designers working outside the dictates of rationalism evolved a liberating and pluralistic design vocabulary from previous decorative styles. Ornament was now returned to its pre-Modern Movement status: a fundamental element of a visually rich culture.

86 **V. Parigi and N. Prina**
Oryx desk, 1970

Ettore Sottsass
Office chair (Synthesis 45),
1970–71

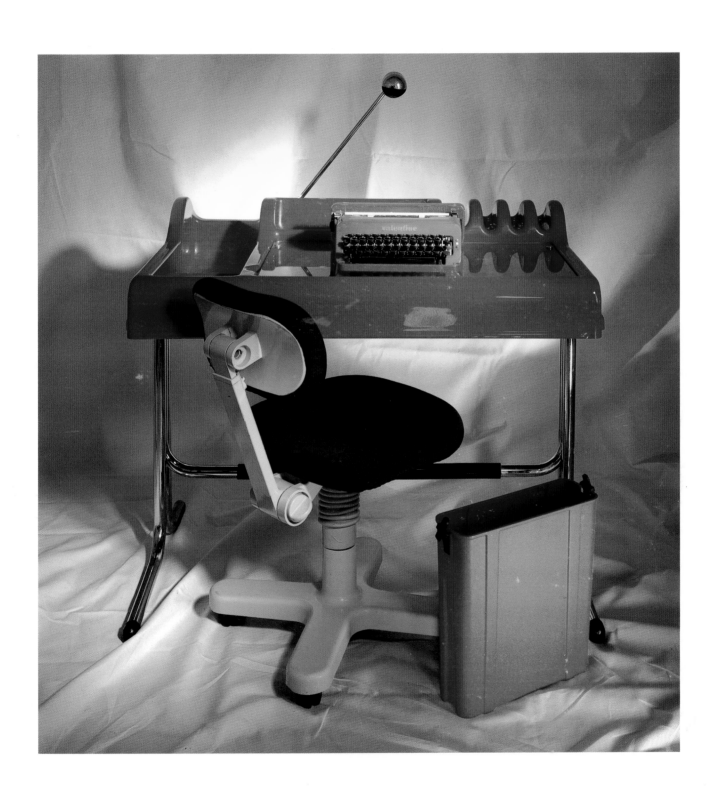

87 **Jonathan De Pas, Donato D'Urbino and Paolo Lomazzi**
Joe chairs, 1970

88 **Jan Ekselius**
Jan sofa and ottoman, *c.* 1970

89 **Eero Aarnio**
Interior with Pony chairs,
c. 1970

90 **Frank Gehry**
    Three nesting chairs, 1972

91 **Etienne-Henri Martin**
    Chauffeuse 1500 chairs, 1970–71

92 (left to right)
    Pierre Paulin
    577 chair, 1967

    Raymond Loewy
    Side cabinet, c. 1967

    Isamu Noguchi
    Table lamp, c. 1960

    Geoffrey Harcourt
    Cleopatra sofa, 1973

    Raymond Loewy
    Sideboard, c. 1967

    Gae Aulenti
    Pileino lamp, 1972

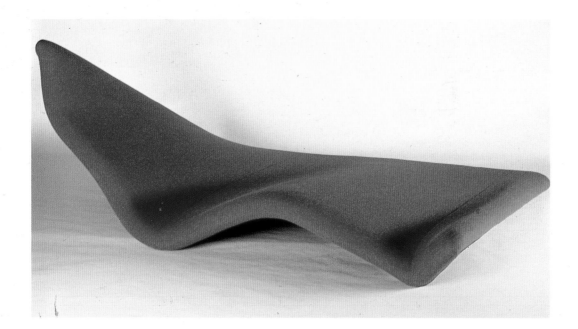

128

97 **Gae Aulenti**
    Aulenti Collection dining table
    and chairs, 1977

98 **Gaetano Pesce**
    Sit Down chairs, 1975

99 **Rodney Kinsman**
    Omkstak chairs, 1971

104 **Alessandro Mendini**
Proust's armchair, 1978

105 **Alessandro Mendini**
Ondoso table, 1980

106 **Alessandro Mendini**
Kandissi sofa, 1980

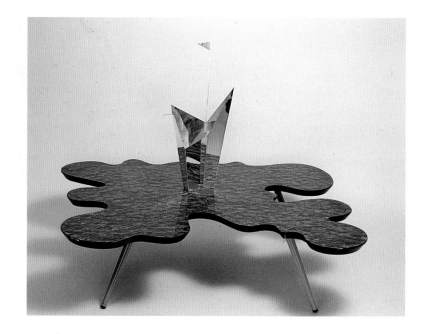

107 **Gaetano Pesce**
Sansone table, 1980

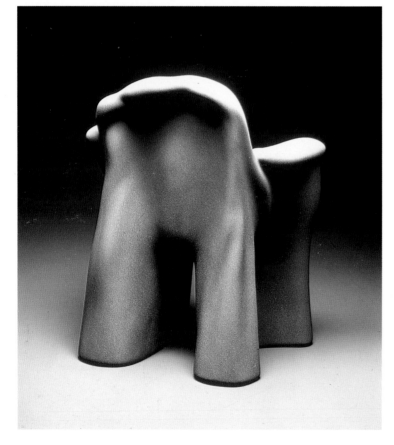

109 **Frank Gehry**
Little Beaver, 1980

110 **Gaetano Pesce**
Dalila chair, 1980

Notes on the furniture

87

V. Parigi, Italian and **Nani Prina**, Italian

Oryx desk, 1970 (86)
Molteni & Co., Italy

Moulded ABS top supported on chromium-plated tubular steel base

86

The moulded top of the Oryx desk incorporates raised and depressed sections for the storage of stationery. Unlike fibreglass, ABS, a non-reinforced thermoplastic, can be easily coloured and has a high-gloss finish on both surfaces.

Ettore Sottsass, Italian (born in Austria), b. 1917

Office chair (Synthesis 45), 1970–71* (86)
Olivetti, Italy

Fabric-covered, foam-filled cushions on injection-moulded ABS frame and base

From 1958, Ettore Sottsass worked as a design consultant for Olivetti and in 1960 he established an additional design studio for the company at Ivrea, near Turin. His commercially successful Valentine typewriter of 1969, manufactured by Olivetti, transformed a utilitarian product into a fashion accessory. The radical Synthesis 45, like the famous typewriter, brought Pop design into the office environment. The chair had a swivel mechanism, adjustable seat heights and the back section folded down so that the chair could be used as a stool. A later die-cast aluminium version, the Z 9/3, was also produced in 1973; both designs are still in production.

Jonathon De Pas, Italian, **Donato D'Urbino**, Italian and **Paolo Lomazzi**, Italian

Joe chairs, 1970* (87)
Poltronova, Italy

Leather-covered moulded polyurethane foam

This design was named after the New York Yankee baseball player and husband of Marilyn Monroe, Joe DiMaggio. It is a costly chair to produce because of the quantity of natural glove leather used. Over-sized and out-of-context furniture such as the Joe chair was inspired partly by the contemporary sculptures of Claes Oldenburg. It is currently produced in several shades of leather.

Jan Ekselius, Swedish

Jan sofa and ottoman, *c.* 1970 (88)
Stendig, USA

Stretch velour fabric covering polyurethane foam moulded directly on to a bent and welded steel-sprung frame

The lithe forms of the Jan sofa and ottoman were made possible by incorporating in the frames' construction a complex latticework of wire and elastic, on to which the foam upholstery could be directly moulded. The velour slipcover was zippered to allow for easy cleaning. A matching chair was also manufactured.

88

Eero Aarnio, Finnish, b. 1932

Interior with Pony chairs, *c.* 1970 (89)
Stendig, USA

89

137

Fabric-covered moulded polyurethane foam

Originally called Mustangs, these toy-like designs were renamed Ponies when they were marketed in the USA by Stendig. Although highly eccentric in form, the Ponies were intended for contract use; a herd of them evidently occupied the boardroom of a corporation based in the mid-west.

Frank Gehry, American (born in Canada), b. 1929

Three nesting chairs, 1972 (90)
Jack Brogan, USA

90

Corrugated laminated cardboard

These nesting chairs form part of Gehry's Easy Edges line of 1972, which consisted of seventeen pieces of cardboard furniture. This material was laminated so that the fluting inside each sheet was placed at ninety degrees from the sheet directly above it and below it, giving the furniture remarkable strength and resilience. The Easy Edges Group was a low-cost, avant-garde design solution which was immediately successful. However, it was manufactured by Jack Brogan for only three months before Gehry, who held the patent, ceased production. The series was reissued briefly by Chiru, USA in 1982.

Etienne-Henri Martin, French

Chauffeuse 1500 chairs, 1970–71 (91)
C.S.T.N. Mangau Atal, France

91

Nylon stretch jersey-covered, foam-upholstered, tubular metal frame

The Chauffeuse 1500 is an uncomplicated and unified design with a flowing, single-piece, wrap-over construction. Like Pierre Paulin's sculptural designs, the chair can accommodate a variety of informal seating positions. The cantilevered form of the

Chauffeuse 1500 allows a degree of flexibility and with its foam upholstery the chair is extremely comfortable.

Interior: Fiell, UK

Pierre Paulin, French, b. 1927

577 chair, 1967* (92)
Artifort, The Netherlands

Stretch jersey-covered, foam-upholstered, tubular steel frame

Pierre Paulin began designing furniture for Artifort in 1958 and became a consultant to the company in 1968. His training in techniques allied to sculpture at the Camondo School were later reflected in his highly fluid furniture designs, such as the serpentine 577, sometimes known as the Tongue Chaise. Its foam upholstery and the ergonomic considerations that partly dictated its design mean that the 577 is extremely comfortable.

Raymond Loewy, American (born in France), 1893–1986

Side cabinet, *c.* 1967 (92)
Doubinski Frères, France for CEI Paris, France

Enamelled wood and metal construction with ABS drawer fronts

92

Raymond Loewy was one of the greatest industrial designers of this century. He was highly prolific throughout his long career, designing furniture, graphics, cars and many other products and was the first designer ever to be featured on the cover of *Time* magazine. The DF2000 series, to which this side cabinet belongs, consisted of a wide variety of case furniture including wardrobes, chests-of-drawers and cabinets. Each design utilized a similar type of drawer front or cupboard door; this form of standardization helped to reduce manufacturing costs. The series was manufactured for Loewy's own design company, CEI Paris, by Doubinski Frères.

Isamu Noguchi, American, 1904–88

Table lamp, *c.* 1960* (92)
Akari, Japan

Mulberry bark paper shade on wire support

Isamu Noguchi designed many *akari* or light-sculptures during his career. Constructed of *washi* papers made from mulberry bark, the lamps evolved from traditional Japanese lanterns and from his experiments in the 1940s with a series of self-illuminated sculptures known as Lunars. The manufacture of *washi* paper was a dying art form in Japan, but through the efforts of Noguchi it has been saved from extinction. The UF1–0 illustrated and many other *akari* are still in production.

Geoffrey Harcourt, British, b. 1935

Cleopatra sofa, 1973* (92)
Artifort, The Netherlands

Stretch jersey-covered, foam-upholstered tubular steel frame supported on metal castors

Geoffrey Harcourt has designed furniture for the Dutch manufacturer Artifort since 1962. The Cleopatra or 248 sofa was inspired by the sculptural designs of Pierre Paulin and can be seen as a homage to Paulin's earlier Ribbon and 577 chairs (*see* colour plates 72 and 92).

Raymond Loewy, American (born in France), 1893–1986

Sideboard, *c.* 1967 (92)
Doubinski Frères, France for CEI Paris, France

Enamelled wood and metal construction with ABS drawer fronts

Loewy wrote: 'Good design keeps the user happy, the manufacturer in the black, and the aesthete unoffended' (*see* Kathryn Hiesinger and George Marcus, *Design Since 1945*, London and Philadelphia 1983, page 220). The sideboard illustrated forms part of the DF2000 series.

Gae Aulenti, Italian, b. 1927

Pileino lamp, 1972 (92)
Artemide, Italy

Moulded plastic construction with chromium-plated metal fittings

Gae Aulenti has achieved international recognition for her work in architecture, interior design, furniture and lighting design. She studied at the Milan polytechnic, where she also taught between 1964 and 1969. The Pileino lamp, like Richard Sapper's Tizio lamp of the same year, can be used as a table lamp or fitted with an optional stand for floor use. The

helmet-like reflector is adjustable so that the intensity and direction of the light can be varied.

The illustration also shows American painter Ron Banks' triptych *Bra Lydin (Ter Raton)*, 1988, mixed media on canvas.

Burkhard Vogtherr, German, b. 1942

Hombre, 1971* (93)
Rosenthal, Germany

93

Rolled-form enamelled metal construction with leather-covered upholstery

Burkhard Vogtherr studied at the schools of art and crafts in Kassel and Wuppertal. The Hombre or Wip chair forms part of his Hombre series designed for Rosenthal in 1971. This chair adjusts to two sitting positions, for working/eating or relaxing/reading. In 1969, Vogtherr received the Federal Gute Form award for his furniture and interior design work.

Achille Castiglioni, Italian, b. 1918

Primate, 1970* (94)
Zanotta, Italy

94

Polystyrene base with vinyl- or leather-covered polyurethane-foam upholstery and stainless steel attachment

The Primate kneeling stool was a highly innovative seating format when it was designed in 1970. The sitter's legs and knees rest on the bottom section while he sits on the upper section. This way of sitting reduces stress on the lower lumber region of the back by partially redistributing the weight on to the legs.

Floris Van den Broecke, British (born in The Netherlands), b. 1945

Chairpiece, 1970–74 (95)
Floris Van den Broecke, UK

Fabric-covered, foam-upholstered, glass-reinforced polyester frame

95

Floris Van den Broecke studied fine art at Arnhem in The Netherlands, going on to study furniture design at the Royal College of Art in London. In 1969 he founded a design partnership with Jane Dillon and Peter Wheeler. The Chairpiece, like other designs by Van den Broecke, alludes to systemized factory production, but has never been put into large-scale production. Van den Broecke's linear furniture designs were partly inspired by the work of his fellow countryman, Gerrit Rietveld.

Studio 65 (Piero Gatti, Cesare Paolini and **Franco Teodoro**; all Italian born 1940s)

Marilyn sofa, 1972* (96)
Gufram, Italy

Stretch nylon jersey-covered, moulded polyurethane foam construction

96

Named after the actress Marilyn Monroe, this sofa is a reinterpretation of Salvador Dali's earlier Mae West sofa of 1936 and as such can be seen to be an early example of redesign, a concept that would be explored by Studio Alchymia. Surrealism, with its anti-design connotations, was a major influence on late 1960s and early 1970s Pop design. The Marilyn is extremely light in weight due to its foam construction and is still in production.

Gae Aulenti, Italian, b. 1927

Aulenti Collection dining table and chairs, 1977* (97)
Knoll International, USA

97

Rolled-form steel frame with polyurethane finish, Dacron-wrapped, foam-upholstered steel seat and backs, laminated or glass table tops

The Aulenti Collection comprises a lounge chair, two- and three-seater sofas, a dining table and five coffee tables. This elegant series intended for the contract market is still in production.

Gaetano Pesce, Italian, b. 1939

Sit Down chairs, 1975* (98)
Cassina, Italy

Polyurethane foam-filled, Dacron-quilted cover over a plywood frame

98

The Sit Down chairs, sofa and ottoman were first produced in 1976 by Cassina. The series can be seen as a comment on the over-upholstered furniture prevalent in the mass-market during the 1970s. Ingeniously constructed, the series did not require costly tooling, for the upholstery itself was used as a mould: the polyurethane foam was poured into the polyester-lined quilted cover where it expanded, filling up the folds of the fabric, except were it met the seat and back sections. This method of production and the use of a mottled printed fabric meant that each chair was slightly different.

Rodney Kinsman, British, b. 1943

Omkstak chairs, 1971* (99)
Bieffeplast, Italy

99

Tubular steel frame with punched sheet steel seat and back

Although it employed an inexpensive method of production, the Omkstak took two years and £20,000 to develop. It is an extremely strong yet relatively light stacking chair that was aimed at both the contract and domestic markets. It can be used indoors or outdoors, making it a truly multi-purpose seating solution and is available in a variety of colours. It is still in production.

Floris Van den Broecke, British (born in The Netherlands), b. 1945

Blue sofa, 1977 (100)
Floris Van den Broecke, UK

Fabric-covered, foam-upholstered aluminium frame

The sofa illustrated, like the Chairpiece (*see* colour plate 94), has not been put into large-scale production.

100

101

Mario Bellini, Italian, b. 1935

Cab sofa, 1977* (101)
Cassina, Italy

Enamelled steel frame upholstered with saddle-stitched leather

The leather upholstery of the Cab armchair, side chair and sofa is zipped on to the steel frames and is available in tan, white and black. During the 1970s, this type of furniture maintained the Italian furniture industry's reputation for high-quality, innovative design.

Floris Van den Broecke, British (born in The Netherlands), b. 1945

English library sofa, 1979 (102)
Floris Van den Broecke, UK

Fabric-covered, foam-upholstered wood frame

102

This sofa was independently manufactured by Van den Broecke, although it was designed so that it could, in theory, be mass-produced. Since 1985, Van den Broecke has been professor of furniture at the Royal College of Art. Recently, his Camber rocking chair of 1990 (co-designed with Jane Dillon and Peter Wheeler as part of the European Design Forum) was put into limited production by the German manufacturer, Thonet.

Fred Scott, British, b. 1942

Supporto armchairs, 1979* (103)
Hille International & Co. Ltd, UK

Foam-upholstered, cast-aluminium construction with gas-cylinder mechanism for raising or lowering the seat

103

The Supporto's form derives almost entirely from ergonomic considerations. Not only was the chair subject to scientific research, Hille also undertook interviews with test users of pre-production models; Scott incorporated the feedback in the final design. The seat and back-rest heights are adjustable and the angle of the back can also be altered. The Supporto is offered in a wide range of variations.

Alessandro Mendini, Italian, b. 1931

Proust's armchair, 1978 (104)
Studio Alchymia, Italy

Existing chair with hand-painted decoration

An early example of redesign, Proust's armchair was included in Studio Alchymia's Bauhaus 1 Collection of 1980. The applied surface decoration was influenced by the work of the Neo-

104

Impressionist painter Georges Seurat, who spent many years researching colour theory. Through redesign, Mendini attempted to illustrate that the intellectual content of a design can derive solely from decorative embellishment: 'good design', he believed, was dead.

Alessandro Mendini, Italian, b. 1931

Ondoso table, 1980 (105)
Studio Alchymia, Italy

Iridescent celluloid top supported on coloured lacquer legs

105

A table designed specifically for Studio Alchymia's Bauhaus 1 Collection of 1980, the Ondoso had an apparently amorphous top that was inspired by the exaggerated free-forms of furniture from the 1950s and, in particular, kitsch. The iridescent celluloid material used produces a shimmering effect and was undoubtedly chosen for its lack of 'good taste': the table intentionally mocks the pretentions of 'good design'.

Alessandro Mendini, Italian, b. 1931

Kandissi sofa, 1980 (106)
Studio Alchymia, Italy

Existing Biedermeier sofa with applied painted wood cut outs

106

Another example of Mendini's redesign, the Kandissi sofa, originally a Biedermeier piece, was applied with painted wooden cut outs inspired by the shapes and colours in Wassily Kandinsky's art. The irreverent use of motifs derived from 'high' art is an attack on the established belief that the fine arts are of a higher intellectual and aesthetic order than the decorative arts. Mendini's work is intentionally confrontational and distances itself, like other designs projected by Studio Alchymia, from consumerism.

Gaetano Pesce, Italian, b. 1939

Sansone table, 1980 (107)
Cassina, Italy

107

Moulded polyester construction

The Sansone was designed by Pesce in collaboration with Jean-Luc Muler and alludes to Samson's love for the treacherous Delilah and his subsequent vengeance: bringing down the columns of the Philistines' temple. Pesce sees this Old Testament story as a parable for the need to free ourselves from social, political and economic doctrines. The Sansone runs counter to industrial standardization, for the production worker determines the shape of the top – the mould is flexible and is neither truly round, square or rectangular – and the combination of colours used. Each table varies slightly and is therefore unique.

Gaetano Pesce, Italian, b. 1939

108

Sunset in New York sofa, 1980* (108)
Cassina, Italy

Fabric-covered, polyurethane foam-upholstered plywood frame with foam and polyester-filled cushions

Sunset in New York is a construction of seven cushions that represent the skyline of a city beneath a giant setting sun. The skyscraper cushions are covered in a two-tone grey, rectangular-patterned fabric, which denotes walls and windows. With this highly eccentric design, Pesce makes reference to the decadence of this North American metropolis.

Frank Gehry, American (born in Canada), b. 1929

Little Beaver, 1980 (109)
Vitra, Switzerland

Laminated corrugated cardboard

109

Like Gehry's earlier Easy Edges series of 1972 (*see* colour plate 90), Little Beaver is constructed of laminated corrugated cardboard. Its edges are left unfinished, as though a beaver has been gnawing at it. Little Beaver was produced in a limited edition with a matching ottoman.

110

Gaetano Pesce, Italian, b. 1939

Dalila chair, 1980 (110)
Cassina, Italy

Moulded, rigid polyurethane with coloured epoxy resin finish

The Dalila series includes an armchair and two side chairs which refer to the Delilah of the Old Testament and which are companion pieces to the Sansone table (*see* colour plate 107). Their melting anthropomorphic forms exploit the fluid qualities of polyurethane. The chairs were available in three surface-coloured epoxy resin finishes: grey, black or brick-red.

1980 to the present day   The eclectic years

Philippe Starck
Sarapis, 1985

Shiro Kuramata
How High the Moon, 1986

Ron Arad
Schizo chair, 1989

5

The 1980s were years of
momentous political change and
renewed economic prosperity,
particularly in the United States and
Europe. After the gloomy years of
recession in the 1970s there was a move
to the political right in both America
and the United Kingdom; a market
economy was now seen as fundamental
to wealth creation. By the middle of the
decade, the economies of America and
most Western European countries were
booming once again. Large amounts of
disposable income were in circulation
and attractive interest rates increased
the availability of credit. Traditional
heavy industries, once a mainstay of
the gross national product of these
economies, had nearly all been replaced
by cleaner, high-tech manufacturing
and the service sector, while the major
financial markets became globally
interrelated through the rapid
development of advanced
communications. In the late 1980s, the
apparent triumph of capitalism, as
transmitted by the increasingly
influential medium of television,
penetrated the Eastern Bloc to dramatic
effect and contributed to the
reunification of Germany and the
democratic rebirth of Poland, Romania
and Czechoslovakia, seemingly
marking the end of the Cold War.

Because of the general upsurge in the
world economy during the 1980s, the
contract furniture market became
much more competitive, while demand
for domestic furnishings also increased
substantially. Throughout the early
years of the decade, these two markets
remained utterly polarized; a
phenomenon that had originated in the
late 1950s. The buoyancy of the
contract furniture market in the 1980s
was a direct result of the spectacular
growth of businesses, especially those
involved in marketing and finance.
These firms realized that through the
decoration of their public and office
spaces they could create a corporate
identity for themselves and that the
advanced furniture systems in which
they invested would also improve the
efficiency of their operations. Because
the contract market was consistently
more profitable than the domestic
furniture market, large manufacturers

such as Fritz Hansen, Cassina and Artifort focused their research and development activities on design solutions for the office environment.

Most of the leading manufacturers who possessed state-of-the-art technology could not provide the flexibility necessary for the production of low-volume, avant-garde domestic design. Mainstream manufacturers, on the other hand, could produce inexpensive domestic furniture for the mass market, but believed that the more anonymous and inoffensive a design the greater its public appeal. This left designers in the 1980s with two options: either they worked for an established manufacturer and designed furniture within a fixed brief, or they independently produced short 'batch' runs of exclusive or 'one-off' furniture.

Most avant-garde designers during this decade were not interested in searching for definitive design solutions that required a huge investment and the long-term commitment of a manufacturer. In the absence of industrial production and in reaction to the rational austerity of the mainstream, the avant-garde created furniture that they could produce themselves or have manufactured in limited quantities by specialized workshops. Using simple, labour-intensive techniques, such as woodcarving, metal-bending and welding, these small-scale enterprises offered greater specialization, thereby allowing the designer more scope for personal creativity. As Charlotte Perriand suggested in 1984: 'I think we can anticipate a return to a more primitive form of craftsmanship – not in the sense of going back to the techniques of the past, but a return to smaller scales of operation, making use of all the potential offered by present and future technology. There may still be a need for manufacture on a large scale to meet some needs, but more and more will be produced by individuals, by artisans. The impact on creativity could be enormous.'[1]

In this period of extraordinary pluralism, where the only characteristic common to the majority of designers was independence from a large-scale manufacturer, post-modernism became the most significant style. Although its origins were primarily architectural, by the early 1980s it was influencing the decorative arts at an international level.

Central to this movement was the Memphis design studio, founded in Milan by Renzo Brugola, Mario and Brunella Godani, Ernesto Gismondi and Fausto Celati in 1981. In common with the radical design groups of the 1970s, Memphis created furniture that ran counter to the accepted tenets of design and culture. Drawing inspiration from either futuristic themes or past decorative styles, designers aligned to Memphis, such as George Sowden (b. 1942), Marco Zanini, Michele De Lucchi, Matheo Thun (b. 1952), Shiro Kuramata (1934–91) and Nathalie Du Pasquier (b. 1957), produced furniture, lighting, textiles, silverware and ceramics. From 1982, Artemide manufactured many of these products for Memphis on a relatively small scale and often in 'multiples', which, like limited-edition sculpture, were priced according to how many were made.

The Italian architect Ettore Sottsass was the designer central to Memphis, playing a guiding role for younger architects such as Marco Zanini and Michele De Lucchi. His work for the studio, together with his earlier designs for Poltronova, 'took the ideological debate about design out of the magazines and integrated it into the designed artifact'.[2] Sottsass was and still is an accomplished publicist and was highly successful in his promotion of Memphis. Sottsass' interest in Pop culture was highly instrumental in his designs and he believed that anti-design should be popularized and made more accessible than it had been in the late 1970s in the work of Studio Alchymia, of which he had been a member. His Memphis designs, such as the Casablanca and Carlton room dividers, employ zoomorphically inspired forms and colourful plastic laminates and were intentionally decadent pieces, which mocked the Modern Movement's canons of 'good taste'. This furniture was anti-functional through its use of decoration, quirkiness of form and towering scale.

Memphis designs were less academic in content and offered a more optimistic forecast of the future than the projections and design predictions of Studio Alchymia. Memphis quoted past styles indirectly, whereas Studio Alchymia used direct quotations in their redesign projects. The name of the group was evidently drawn from a Bob Dylan record of 1966, 'Stuck inside of Mobile with the Memphis Blues Again', which the members of Memphis played repeatedly at a group meeting. The name is extremely apt, for it makes reference to both the ancient Egyptian capital of culture and the Tennessee birthplace of Elvis Presley. This mixing of references and 'double-coding' was the predominant subject matter of Memphis designs; eclecticism in single objects answering Jencks' call for hybrid themes. Unlike their radical predecessors, they did not spurn the advanced technology gained through the rationalism of the postwar furniture industry. Most Memphis furniture, especially that designed by Sottsass, utilized state-of-the-art plastic laminates, often decorated with motifs inspired by Pop art and, in Michele De Lucchi's case, Op Art. The vibrancy of colours, the eccentricity of form and applied decoration were evolved from a working knowledge of modernism, which was subsequently rejected, as Penny Sparke suggests: 'Memphis succeeded not only in suggesting a new philosophical base for design – "it is a widespread drive to attain renewal, a genetic and spontaneous mutation of chromosomes of international design" – but in providing a new iconography for it as well.'[3]

Memphis furniture captured the attention of the world's press at the Milan Furniture Fair of 1981, with its bright colours, primary shapes (cubes, cones, pyramids, spheres) and blatant anti-design statement. Not only did it create a high visual impact, but it also represented an intellectually plausible alternative to rationalism. By obliquely drawing inspiration from former decorative styles, Memphis was able to achieve an independent visual vocabulary and a clear identity.

Other designers, such as Robert Venturi, Hans Hollein and Michael Graves (b. 1934), were also producing post-modern furniture in this period. Robert Venturi's series of chairs manufactured by Knoll International could almost be dubbed 'Neo-Pop', with their bright paint finishes and cardboard cut-out look. Roy Lichtenstein's comic-strip references were another inspiration for the use of dotted paint finishes that emphasized the two-dimensionality of surfaces. Plastic laminates were particularly favoured not only for their association with kitsch, but also for, as Sottsass describes it, their 'lack of culture'.

Post-modern furniture was never intended to possess the built-in obsolescence associated with Pop designs such as Peter Murdoch's Child's chair of 1963, however. It was a reaction against the industrially inspired style of High-Tech and the other supremely functional furniture forms that were prevalent in the mass market during the 1970s. Post-modern designers attempted to divorce industry from design and related it more to fine art. Unlike 1970s mainstream design, post-modernism drew inspiration from architecture and fine art rather than from functionalism and consumerism. In its approach to furniture design, styling, rather than rationalism or pure design, was paramount. Surrealism and kitsch were also primary influences on the movement. Indeed, important precursors of post-modernism, Carlo Mollino, Piero Fornasetti, Salvador Dali and Antoni y Cornet Gaudí (1852–1926) were seen as early exponents of high-quality kitsch who had opposed modernism. Andrea Branzi writes of Mollino: 'With great professionalism and lack of prudence, he had been the first person in Italy to penetrate deep into the quagmire of kitsch, though this was always offset by the precision and excellence of his design and by a considerable force of expression. He put forward, without misgivings, a Hollywood-style alternative to the architectural moralism of the country.'[4]

American and British post-modern designers tended to cull inspiration from historicism during the 1980s, while their colleagues from Japan, such as Shiro Kuramata and Arata Isozaki,

George Sowden
Oberoy chair, 1981

and those from the Continent, preferred futuristic themes. The post-modern architect-designers from the USA and the UK playfully reinterpreted traditional design motifs, reintroducing symbolism, colour and most importantly ornament for its own sake. Through the use of traditional architectural motifs and design formats, they created novel designs which were open to the influence of all period styles. The designers based in America, such as Robert Venturi and Michael Graves, are sometimes referred to as post-modern Classicists, for they frequently reinterpreted classical themes. They revelled in the use of exuberant colour, ornament and decoration derived from historic styles, while at the same time emphasizing the two-dimensionality of surfaces. Indeed, much post-modern design can be seen as reminiscent – in spirit, at least – of the furniture shown at London's Great Exhibition of 1851, which displayed an abundant use of historicism and revivalism.

Andrea Branzi, meanwhile, who had praised Carlo Mollino's detachment from rational, mainstream design, was involved not only in the work of Memphis, but also in his own continuing explorations of anti-design. His work centred increasingly in the early 1980s on the Domus Academy in Milan. The Academy, which was set up in 1982, encouraged designers such as Branzi to carry out their innovative work within a disciplined, academic environment, promoting the study of cultural and social issues. Branzi's concept of the 'soft' elements of furniture design related to the sensory experiences involved in the use of furniture, for example, sound, smell and lighting, as well as the obvious tactile experience.

The 'Craft Revival', meanwhile, which had gained momentum from its beginnings in the 1970s, continued throughout the 1980s with designers such as Wendell Castle in the United States and John Makepeace (b. 1939) in the United Kingdom re-establishing 'the artisan-traditions of furniture-making rather in the manner of the nineteenth-century Arts and Crafts movement'.[5]

John Makepeace
Oak dining chairs, 1983

Craft furniture design had been well established, if only as a minority style, since the end of the Second World War. In America, the work of designers such as George Nakashima harked back to the Shaker furniture of the nineteenth century. The simple beauty of Shaker design and the pure ideals that lay behind it provided the inspiration for early craft-oriented pieces.

By the early 1980s, however, Craft Revival furniture had departed from this arts and crafts approach. Wendell Castle, whose work in the 1970s was highly organic in form, turned in the 1980s to more figurative forms of design, in accordance with the general trend of post-modernist ideology. The figurative phase of his work even included minutely perfect *trompe-l'oeil* carvings of clothes draped over furniture. Much of his later work appears to have been carved from a solid piece of wood, whereas, in fact, Castle bonds together blocks of wood of appropriate sizes.

Castle has never intended that his work should be produced by machine; in common with other Craft Revival designers, he would argue, quite rightly, that a machine could not even come close to matching the technical and artistic virtuosity of his handcrafted work. Indeed, the technical and artistic accomplishment of his work has tended to overwhelm considerations of function, with the result that many consider it to be as much sculpture as furniture.

The British Craft Revival movement includes designers such as Richard La Trobe Bateman, Rupert Williamson and Martin Grierson, but it is John Makepeace who is the most prominent. Makepeace's Ebony and Nickel-Silver chair of 1978 is a refined example of Craft Revival design. Laboriously time-consuming to construct, this chair utilizes over two thousand pieces of ebony and draws on both Gothic and Art Nouveau sources of inspiration for its form and decorative detail. The use of high-quality materials and labour-intensive techniques meant that Craft Revival furniture remained extremely expensive in both Britain and America, and because of this it has had virtually no effect on the mass market.

Designers associated with the Craft Revival frequently allude to traditional forms or to post-modern themes. The reliance on virtuoso cabinet-making skills and beautiful woods has often been detrimental to the advancement of progressive design; Craft Revival furniture is not radical or subversive. However, in recent years Makepeace's school, at Parnham House in Dorset (founded in 1977), has been promoting a harmonious balance of design and craftsmanship which has resulted in highly accomplished designs, such as Konstantin Grcic's 1990 Briol chair.

The element of Craft Revival design that places function low on its list of priorities is perhaps best exemplified by the work of Fred Baier; the exhibition of his work at the Crafts Council in 1990 included furniture whose function was barely discernible. Such furniture, together with the masterly, highly aesthetic work of designers like John Makepeace and Wendell Castle, blurs the distinction between art and craft in a way that suggests, perhaps, that Craft Revival furniture is more subversive than it first appears.

A sophisticated style characterized by a delicate synthesis of design and styling also emerged in the 1980s. Identified as 'Late Modern' by Michael Collins and 'Neo-Modern' by Penny Sparke, this exceptionally elegant yet functional approach to design bears a similarity of spirit to the Postwar International Style. Designers such as Philippe Starck (b. 1949), Matthew Hilton (b. 1957) and Jasper Morrison (b. 1959) have created highly successful careers for themselves designing sleekly profiled furniture that exemplifies the Late Modern aesthetic.

Philippe Starck is an enigmatic figure who has consistently commanded the attentions of the world press. His enthusiasm for his own work is endearing while his sheer productivity is startling. Few designers have been so celebrated; he has achieved international pre-eminence, elevating the status of designer to one of superstar. Starck began his career by designing a collection of inflatable furniture sponsored by French designer Nguyen Manh Khan'h's company, Quasar. He worked later, for a brief period, in the Pierre Cardin studio as design director, creating sixty-five pieces of furniture. In 1980 he formed his own company, Starck Products, and it was not long before he was designing for major manufacturers such as Flos, Driade and Kartell. Starck first came to prominence in 1981, when he was one of eight designers selected to refurbish and design furniture for apartments in the Elysée Palace. Believing that aesthetics are an essential function of furniture, his work is imbued with an unmistakable Parisian chic and a personal symbolism that does not deny historical styles or future technology. Starck creates individual personalities for his designs through the deliberate use of evocative titles, such as, Dr Bloodmoney, Nina Freed and Miss Dorn. He is highly prolific and can create elegant designs on paper in a matter of minutes. Often leaving the technical problems of how a design is to be realized to the manufacturer, he is one of the few designers who is able keep up with the perpetual demand for new and exciting products. By the early 1980s, his enormously influential furniture was being widely mimicked; these imitations eventually culminated in what became known as 'Matt Black' kitsch: low-grade interpretations of Late Modern furniture, destined for the mass market.

Starck's sensitivity to the functional requirements of mass-produced furniture can be seen in his Café Costes chair, designed in 1984. Initially, this three legged 'tub' chair was designed site specific for a fashionable Parisian café, but it is now inexpensively mass-produced by the Italian manufacturer Baleri. Another highly successful mass-produced design, the Dr Glob stacking chair, was designed by Starck on a Paris–Tokyo flight for the Milan Furniture Fair of 1988. Dr Glob is constructed of injection-moulded polypropylene and steel tubing and is manufactured by Kartell. Defending his use of plastic, which he describes as 'an aristocratic material', Starck insists: 'Plastic is the only real ecological answer now. It is impossible to cut down a tree just to put your ass on it. In the next twenty years we will know that animals have a soul, and in the

Matthew Hilton
Antelope table, 1987

next 200 years, I'm sure we will discover that trees have a soul too. I'm sure that petrol has no soul. I'm joking, but certain things are important nevertheless.'[6] Joke or not, Starck, like all designers working in the product- and furniture-design industries in the late twentieth century, has to consider ecological issues. The potential for recycling would suggest that plastic is ecologically sound if used responsibly for durable products.

Because 'one-off' and limited-edition furniture is not subject to the constraints of mass production, designers working in this area are able to express themselves more freely through designs that employ a wide variety of forms and materials. Since the latter half of the decade, the market for this exclusive furniture has flourished, with specialist galleries exhibiting the work of independent designers such as Ron Arad (b. 1951), Tom Dixon, André Dubreuil and Danny Lane. Richard Rogers (b. 1933) has described this type of anti-design furniture as 'usable artwork',[7] identifying its aesthetic intentions. As Deyan Sudjic explains: 'A better way of understanding what has happened to what may best be called industrial design, out of all possible definitions of design, is to see its present avant-garde manifestations not just as a temporary outbreak of iconoclasm, but more as the kind of mutation that overtook art following the discovery of photography. Representational painting was no longer the only option for the artist. Photography had usurped some of the representational responsibilities of painting, freeing the artist to do other things. In the same way, the act of creating, that is to say designing, a form for an everyday object can retain its power, even when it is not used as the prelude for the manufacture of an artifact designed to be sold at a price, in large numbers. To pursue the analogy, in time photography itself developed aspirations to achieving the status and the attention afforded to art, and what had originally been seen as a skill became something else.'[8]

Ron Arad and Danny Lane do not attempt to turn design into art but rather redefine the generally accepted rationalist definition of 'design'. Their work appeals to our emotions, which they exploit through the tactile and visual qualities of their materials. Using glass and sheet steel with lyrical fluency, they transform everyday materials into beautiful, if not particularly functional, furniture.

In 1981, Ron Arad opened his One Off showroom in Covent Garden as a means of exhibiting his own furniture design, as well as that by Danny Lane and Tom Dixon. Incorporating both studio and workshop in one facility was a new concept in furniture retailing; One Off functioned more as a forum for promoting new ideas than as a commercially run gallery. In the early 1980s, the work produced by these designers was characterized by the use of salvaged objects: in Arad's case, Rover car seats, while Dixon used frying pans and manhole covers. These were 'rough and ready' constructions which were consciously distanced from mass-produced furniture – Arad's concrete-encased stereo speakers were in direct opposition to the 'good forms' of audio equipment produced by companies such as Bang & Olufson. Inspired by Dada, Arad believes that Duchamp rendered the objects he adapted for his readymades useless by turning them into art. Arad's work, like the Castiglioni brothers' earlier 'readymade' furniture, transforms rather than destroys the material function of found objects.

Independent avant-garde designers such as Arad, Lane, Dixon and Dubreuil, as well as Elisabeth Garouste and Mattia Bonetti, produce limited furniture design which purposely appears handmade. It conveys a sense of 'spontaneous creativity' and reflects the personality of the creator. These designers have not transposed furniture into art, but aim specifically to create poetic, three-dimensional design which possesses aesthetic characteristics similar to those of painting and sculpture.

Although Floris Van den Broecke (b. 1945) and Zaha Hadid also produce limited furniture designs, their intentions are very different from those of the One Off designers. Trained in the rationalist tradition, they design furniture with the potential for large-scale production in an attempt to negotiate a contract with a manufacturer. Van den Broecke writes: 'At the time when I trained, I would perhaps have liked to end up working as a staff designer for a large-scale manufacturer. But the problem, then as now, is that there are so few firms that actually employ furniture designers. One has to make things oneself, if one is going to see them produced at all. My work has always speculated on the possibilities of batch production, and it has never emphasised the quality of making.'[9] Furniture designed by Hadid and Van den Broecke is highly finished and alludes to systemized factory production. Similarly, prototypical designs, such as John Greed's 1991 Mocean chair and Mark Robson's GRP chair, are intended for a process of production. The Mocean chair, in fact, exploits one of the newest materials available to furniture designers, that is, carbon fibre. This extraordinary fibre facilitates the production of very light but extremely strong pieces of furniture. The fact that the manufacture of this form of prototype furniture is often limited, however, means that high costs are unavoidable.

Throughout the 1980s and continuing into the 1990s, the growing public interest in designed products was fuelled by the emergence of numerous interiors and lifestyle magazines. Avant-garde furniture design was increasingly in demand, for it symbolized the spirit of the times and expressed individualism. A wide variety of this new furniture, diverse in its styling and mainly created outside the industrial process, was now available to a more affluent clientele, which was willing to invest in progressive design that possessed a fashionable cachet. The exclusive, one-off furniture created during this period often had only a symbolic affinity with functionalism. While it commonly appeared sculptural and highly aesthetic, it cannot be considered sculpture – fine art is created according to a different, not higher, set of aesthetics.

John Greed
Mocean chair, 1991

III **Toshiyuki Kita**
Wink chair, 1980

As we approach the turn of the century, design has become a critical issue with global implications. Related to industry and therefore the environment, the success or failure of design will ultimately affect the quality of our lives. In a world that cannot sustain endless industrial growth, designers and manufacturers must produce better designed and more ecologically efficient products. Rampant consumerism will have to be controlled and an effective method of encouraging this is the promotion of rational design. History has indicated, however, that although the public may accept the necessity for 'good design' it will not tolerate the dictation of taste. Education is the best means of ensuring the public's understanding and acceptance of socially responsible design.

Since the Second World War, the cycles of rationalism and anti-rationalism have coincided with the decline and growth of the western world's economy. In the twenty-first century, social, political and economic concerns will undoubtedly prompt decorative styles, but the environment will play a more important role and, by necessity, effect the dominance of rational design. At a seminar entitled 'Synthetic Visions' at the Royal College of Art in 1990, several eminent designers, including Daniel Weil and Michele De Lucchi, concluded that new technology and synthetic materials must be exploited for the manufacture of durable products. In the 1960s, the environmentally unsound anti-design ethic of expendability was often expressed in plastic, a fundamentally non-disposable material. The rational use of plastics in the furniture industry, however, may yet prove ecologically justifiable should the necessary incentives be provided for systems of effective recycling. Having met the challenges of the past, designers must now be given the freedom to create the classic design of the future and fulfil the pressing environmental needs of our rapidly changing world.

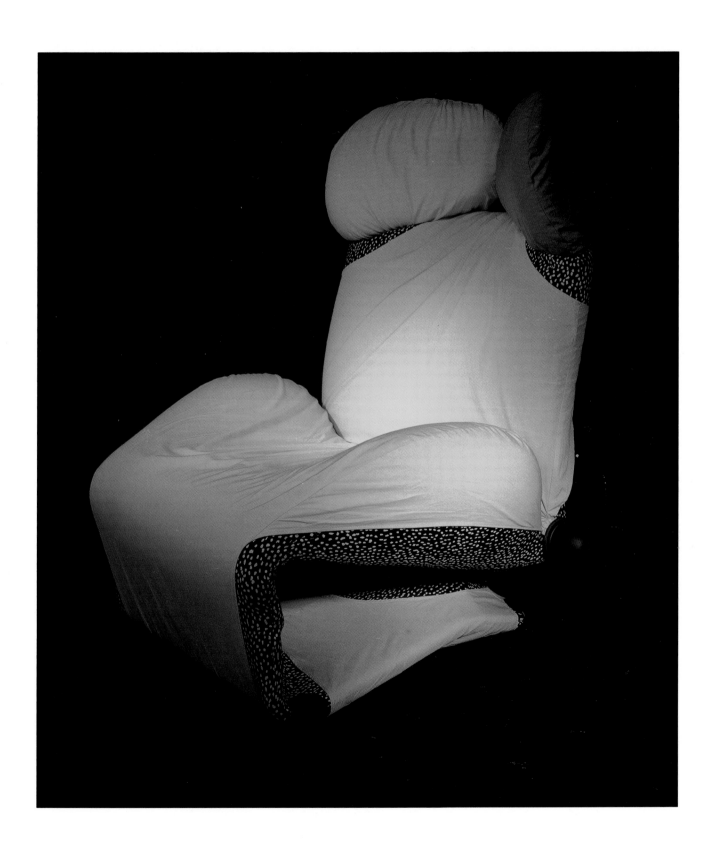

112 **Ettore Sottsass**
Casablanca, 1981

113 **George Sowden**
Antibes, 1981

114 **Ettore Sottsass**
Carlton, 1981

115 **Peter Shire**
Bel Air armchair, 1982

116 **Peter Shire**
Brazil table, 1981

117 **Hans Hollein**
Mitzi, 1981

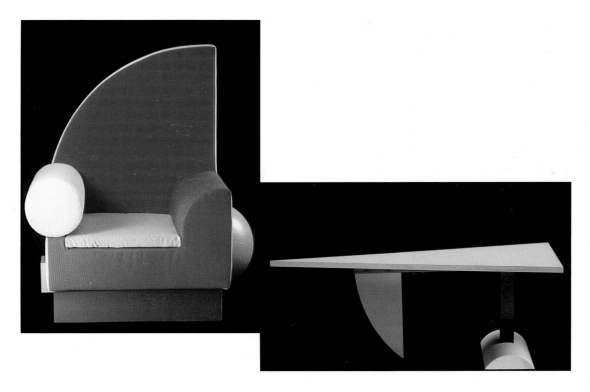

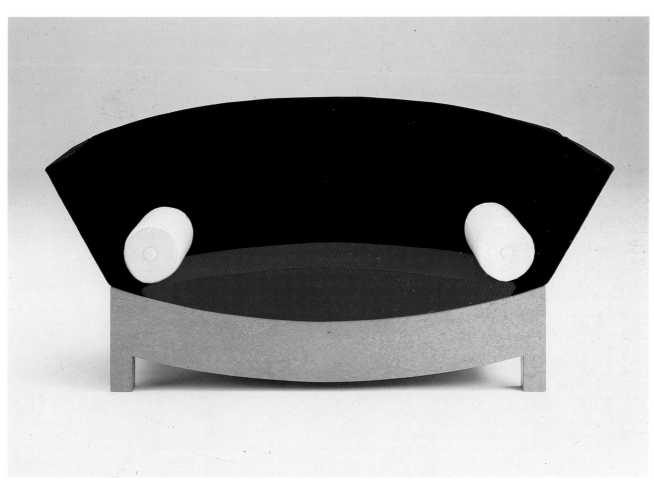

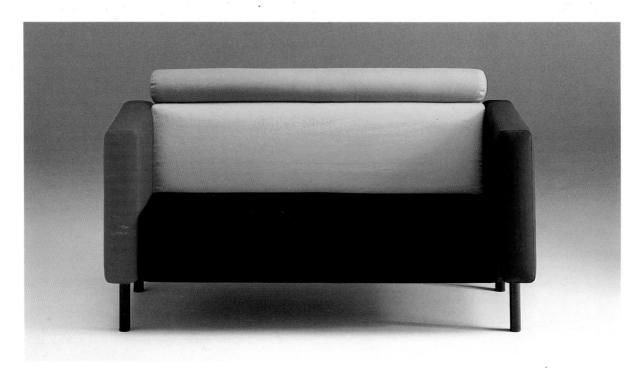

118 **Ettore Sottsass**
Westside Collection, 1983

119 **Stefano Casciani**
Albertina sofa, 1984

120 **Robert Venturi**
Venturi Collection, 1984

121 **Borek Sipek**
Ernst und Guduld chair, 1988

122 **Philippe Starck**
Dr Glob chairs, 1988

123 **Danny Lane**
Chaise Longhi, 1988

124 **John Makepeace**
Serving table, 1986

125 **Nigel Coates**
Genie stool, 1988

126 **Richard Artschwager**
Chair/Chair, 1986–87

127 **Borek Sipek**
Basket Weave chair, 1988

128 **André Dubreuil**
Spine chair, 1988

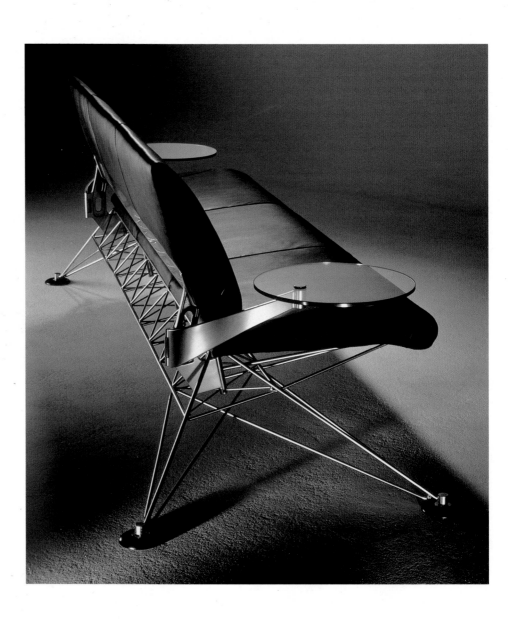

129 **Danny Lane**
Oisin table, 1988

130 **Danny Lane**
Atlas table, 1988

131 **Roy Fleetwood**
Wing sofa, 1988

132 **Danny Lane**
Solomon chair and table, 1988

133 **Ron Arad**
Big Easy Red Volume 1, 1989

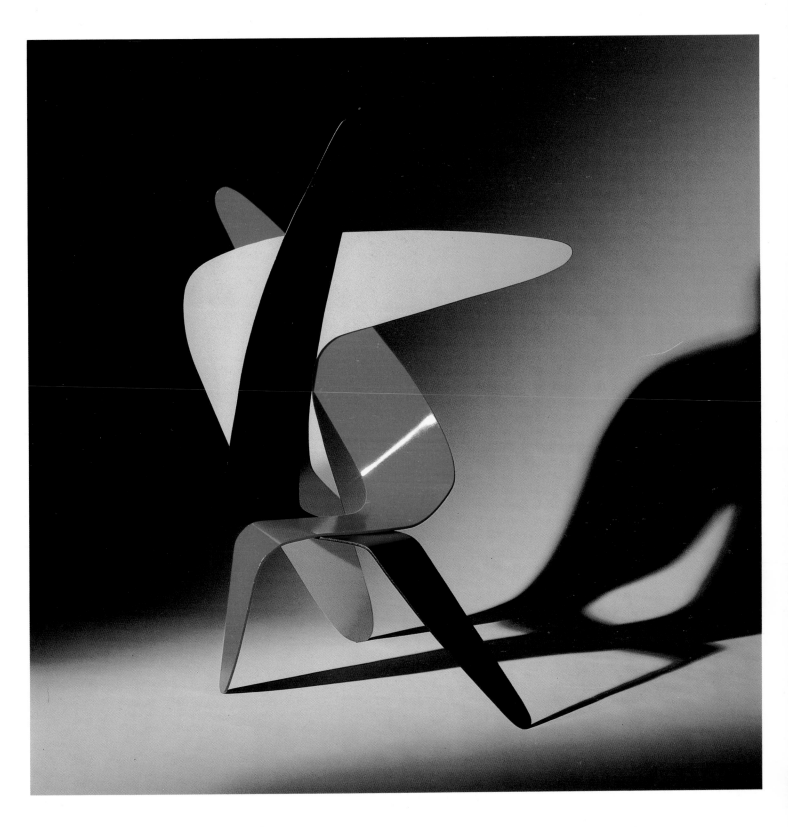

134 **Sue Golden**
Boomerang chair, 1989

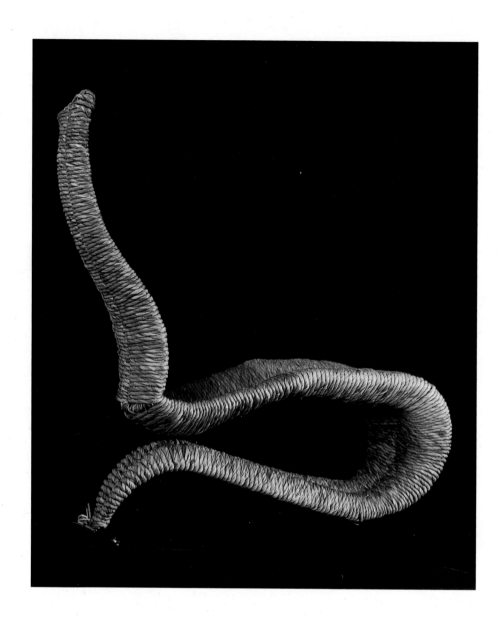

135 **Tom Dixon**
Chaise (Rush), 1990

136 **Tom Dixon**
S chairs, 1988

137 **Fred Baier**
Desk, 1989

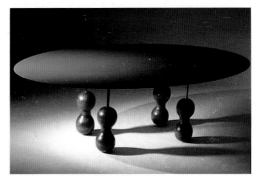

138 **Mark Robson**
GRP chairs, 1989

139 **Elisabeth Garouste and Mattia Bonetti**
Star sofa, *c.* 1988

140 **Marco Zanuso Jr**
Table, 1989

141 **Elisabeth Garouste and Mattia Bonetti**
Imperial chair, *c.* 1988

142 **Martin Szekely**
Liberata table, 1989

143 **Elisabeth Garouste and Mattia Bonetti**
Afrika table, 1990

144 **Konstantin Grcic**
Armchair and side chair, 1990

Notes on the furniture

Toshiyuki Kita, Japanese, b. 1942

Wink chair, 1980* (111)
Cassina, Italy

Expanded polyurethane foam injected over a welded steel armature, padded with 'Dacron' fibrefill and upholstered in fabric, leather or vinyl

111

Toshiyuki Kita studied at the University of Design, Osaka, where in 1964 he opened his own design firm. Having worked in Italy, Kita designs furniture that combines traditional Japanese and European influences. The Wink's novel headrest is divided into two sections which can be independently adjusted and the zipper-fastened covering can be easily removed for cleaning. It is currently in production and is available in a variety of colour combinations.

Ettore Sottsass, Italian (born in Austria), b. 1917

Casablanca, 1981
Memphis, Italy

112

Plastic laminate on wood carcase

Sottsass' Memphis designs, such as the Casablanca and the Carlton Room Divider, were intentionally decadent pieces that mocked the Modern Movement's canons of 'good taste'. The surfaces of the colourful plastic laminates used by Memphis were decorated with patterns of the designers'

own making; these state-of-the-art materials were manufactured by Abet Laminati.

George Sowden, British, b. 1942

Antibes, 1981 (113)
Memphis, Italy

Plastic laminate on wood carcase

British expatriate George Sowden was a member of Ettore Sottsass' Olivetti studio and later became one of the founding members of Memphis. Often working in collaboration with his French partner Nathalie Du Pasquier, Sowden contributed some of the less exaggerated forms to Memphis' first few collections, including the Antibes display cabinet and the large Luxor closet of 1982, as well as chairs, clocks, carpets and watches. The brightly coloured Abet plastic laminate used on Antibes was designed by Sowden and is decorated on the sides with a pattern of broken fragments.

113

114

Ettore Sottsass, Italian (born in Austria), b. 1917

Carlton, 1981 (114)
Memphis, Italy

Plastic laminate on wood carcase

This room divider/storage unit with its bright colours, quirkiness of form and towering scale demands to be isolated from other pieces of furniture in an interior. Creating a high visual impact, the Carlton was conceived not only to be decorative, but also to hold or store books and objects. Although the materials it employs are relatively inexpensive, the labour-intensive construction of Memphis furniture makes it expensive to produce.

Peter Shire, American, b. 1947

Bel Air armchair, 1982 (115)
Memphis, Italy

Wood frame with fabric-covered foam upholstery

American designer Peter Shire studied at the Chovinard Institute of Art and from 1981 has designed furniture and ceramics for Memphis. Born in Los Angeles, Shire creates furniture that expresses the Californian 'funk aesthetic', which is characterized by hot colours and bold asymmetrical forms. The Bel Air armchair, like his ceramics, represents a collection of different shapes and surfaces which have been assembled to form a whole.

115

116

Peter Shire, American, b. 1947

Brazil table, 1981 (116)
Memphis, Italy

Enamelled and lacquered wood

Shire was the only non-architect among the Memphis designers. With a background in craft, he nonetheless possessed a strong affinity for architecture and his work was seen to cross the barriers between fine art and design. Shire's strikingly sculptural Brazil table is one of his better known furniture designs. The green and yellow colours were inspired by the Brazilian flag and, like his Bel Air chair (*see* colour plate 115), the table is a construction of boldly formed individual shapes.

Hans Hollein, Austrian, b. 1934

Mitzi, 1981 (117)
Poltronova, Italy

117

Fabric-covered foam upholstery on wood frame with blond root-wood face veneer

Hollein's furniture designs draw their inspiration from styles as diverse as Neo-Classicism and Art Deco; the Mitzi sofa makes reference to Biedermeier. A variation of this well-proportioned sofa is available with a printed pattern of large pink flowers and lily pads. A low, octagonal, Biedermeier-influenced blond wood table was also designed to match either sofa.

Ettore Sottsass, Italian (born in Austria), b. 1917

Westside Collection, 1983 (118)
Knoll International, USA

Fabric-covered, moulded polyurethane foam upholstery on steel frame with ivory-finished or ebonized steel legs

118

The Westside Collection comprises a lounge chair, a two-person and a three-person sofa and is a companion series to the Eastside Collection. In these designs, Sottsass has employed a language of energy: liberating colour, divorced geometrical forms and deformed structure. He uses colour to upset traditional contours, decoration to upset static structures and machine-age products to upset prejudices against synthetic materials.

Stefano Casciani, Italian, b. 1965

Albertina sofa, 1984 (119)
Zanotta, Italy

Four fabric- or leather-covered, foam-upholstered moulded sections on plywood frame with brushed steel legs

119

Casciani trained in architecture and industrial design. He designed the Albertina sofa with the intention of low-cost mass production. Although the sofa is small, it has a comfortable seating area.

120

Robert Venturi, American, b. 1925

Venturi Collection, 1984 (120)
Knoll International, USA

Moulded and plastic-laminated plywood

Robert Venturi's collection of furniture manufactured by Knoll International could almost be dubbed Neo-Pop, with its bright paint finishes and 'cardboard cutout' look. Roy Lichtenstein's comic-strip references were another inspiration for the use of blocked-in, coloured finishes, which emphasized that the surfaces were two-dimensional. The collection comprises a sofa, nine chairs and two tables. The nine chairs are named after individual period styles, the essences of which are expressed through the chairs' ornament: Queen Anne, Gothic(k), Chippendale, Hepplewhite, Sheraton, Empire, Biedermeier, Art Nouveau and Art Deco.

Borek Sipek, Czech, b. 1949

Ernst und Guduld chair, 1988 (121)
Neotu, France

Bird's-eye maple, stained and ebonized sycamore

This chair, like Sipek's basket weave chairs, was influenced by the tribal art of the Philippines, where he spent some time.

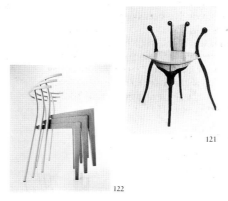
121
122

Philippe Starck, French, b. 1949

Dr Glob chairs, 1988 (122)
Kartell, Italy

Injection-moulded polypropylene and steel tubing

Stark is reassessing his output and taking a more considered approach to design: 'My main ambition – no production – this year (1990) has been to design with NO STYLE. For many years we all sought style. Now we need discretion . . . . With a good product, there is no obligation to show its design' (*see* M. Bellini, *The International Design Yearbook 1990–1991*, London 1990, page 89).

Danny Lane, British (born in America), b. 1955

Chaise Longhi, 1988 (123)
Danny Lane, UK

Wood and glass construction

123

Creating unique, one-off furniture primarily in glass, Lane approaches his work intuitively. He is uninterested in comfort and utility, preferring expression over functionalism: sitting – or reclining, as is the case with Chaise Longhi – on a glass surface runs counter to the user's instincts and instils an uneasy sense of vulnerability.

John Makepeace, British, b. 1939

Serving table, 1986 (124)
John Makepeace, UK

Scrubbed burr oak and burr elm construction

124

The application of high-quality materials and labour-intensive techniques has meant that Craft Revival furniture, such as Makepeace's Serving table, remains highly exclusive and extremely expensive.

Nigel Coates, British, b. 1949

Genie stool, 1988 (125)
Branson Coates Architecture, UK

Carved, sandblasted, solid ash seat on twisted mild steel legs

125

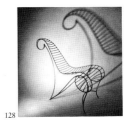

128

The Genie stool is carved in two parts, which are joined like human pelvic bones and hover above the steel base. Because of the forward tilt of the seat, and the saddle effect of the wooden pommel, sitting on it straightens and energizes the spine.

Richard Artschwager, American, b. 1924

Chair/Chair, 1986–87 (126)
Vitra, Switzerland

Leather-covered foam upholstery on a bent wood frame

Although Richard Artschwager has been associated with the Pop Art and Minimal Art movements of the 1960s and early 1970s, he is an enigmatic figure whose creative output is constantly evolving. Artschwager considers his work to be both sculpture and furniture; it certainly defies easy categorization. The Chair/Chair's name expresses the purpose of the design, which is to function as an inviting two-person seat.

126

127

Borek Sipek, Czech, b. 1949

Basket Weave chair, 1988 (127)
Driade, Italy

Basket weave over wood frame

Sipek's sculptural and organic Basket Weave series of chairs was first launched at the Milan Furniture Fair of 1988. More interested in primitive cultural references than functionalism, Sipek intentionally designs counter to the traditions of pure design and the industrial process.

André Dubreuil, British (born in France), b. 1951

Spine chair, 1988* (128)
A. D. Decorative Arts Ltd, UK

Bent and welded mild steel

André Dubreuil works primarily in metal, producing furniture in the spirit of eighteenth-century French *ébénistes* and of Emile Jacques Ruhlmann. Also drawing inspiration from Rococo and Art Deco, his lyrical and organic designs are intended to be full of life, while not appearing to be salvaged. The Spine chair, one of his best-known pieces of furniture, is in limited production: each chair is individually constructed by a blacksmith in Dubreuil's native Dordogne, so each is slightly different. Dubreuil prefers the flexibility and scope for personal creativity that exclusive and small-scale methods of operation provide.

Danny Lane, British (born in America), b. 1955

Oisin table, 1988 (129)
Danny Lane, UK

Hand-forged steel base supporting clear plate-glass top

Because one-off furniture is created outside any production constraint, it can freely express the designer's spontaneous creativity. Neo-Romantic anti-design such as the Oisin table appeals to our emotions, through the fluent and lyrical use of tactile and visually appealing materials.

129

130

Danny Lane, British (born in America), b. 1955

Atlas table, 1988 (130)
Fiam, Italy

Clear float-glass legs with stainless steel studding, supporting plate-glass top

Lane believes that his personality and attitude towards design will be projected through his distinctive furniture: 'The architecture of my pieces is constructed around a respect for materials, function and aesthetic performance. I have compressors, sandblasters, welders, grinders and large sheets of glass, but the most important instruments are myself and the team' (*see* M. Bellini, *The International Design Yearbook 1990–1991*, London 1990, page 97).

Roy Fleetwood, British, b. 1946

Wing sofa, 1988
Vitra, Switzerland

131

Leather-covered foam upholstery on steel frame

Architect Roy Fleetwood uses the forms and construction principles of High-Tech architecture to create furniture with a fascinating visual lightness. The filigree base of the Wing sofa resembles the span of a bridge: the seat curves outwards while the back, which resembles an aircraft wing, appears to float.

Danny Lane, British (born in America), b. 1955

132

Solomon chair and table, 1988 (132)
Danny Lane, UK

Clear and sandblasted float glass with stainless steel studding, the table with etched marble shelf

Using a system of carefully controlled 'random' breakage and fracture, Lane

builds up pieces such as these in layers of float glass, which are secured with stainless steel studs and glue. The edges of each glass component are bevelled and ground so as to minimize the risk of injury. Through these visually tenuous yet intriguing constructions, Lane's intention has been to create poetic furniture which possesses aesthetic characteristics similar to those of painting and sculpture.

Ron Arad, British (born in Israel), b. 1951

Big Easy Red Volume 1, 1989 (133)
Moroso, Italy for One Off Ltd, UK

Vinyl upholstery over bent and welded mild steel

Ron Arad's furniture is suffused with complicated references to major precedents in art history, in particular Dada. Unlike Marcel Duchamp's 'readymade' works of art, however, Arad's early salvaged and recycled Rover car seats transform rather than destroy the material function of found objects. The Big Easy Red Volume 1 evolved from the Big Easy Collection; although these chairs are cut from similar patterns, each model from the series retains an individual personality.

133

134

Sue Golden, British

Boomerang chair, 1989
S. Golden for Fiell, UK

Welded and enamelled bent aluminium construction

Working in a variety of materials and finishes, Sue Golden looks to primitive art as a source of inspiration. With an emphasis on shape and colour, the simple forms of her sculptural furniture designs give them a powerful presence. Golden's Boomerang chair, with obvious aboriginal influences, appears an uncomplicated construction until inspected closely. Like a Calder sculpture, it is a complex assemblage of elementary shapes and each surface is finished with a different texture.

Tom Dixon, British, b. 1959

Chaise (Rush), 1990 (135)
Dixon P.I.D., UK

Woven rush on a bent, mild steel frame

Tom Dixon, like Ron Arad and André Dubreuil, works from his own studio with a staff of a few assistants producing highly individual furniture that expresses his own interests and spontaneous creativity. He is a self-taught metal worker, who earlier in his career designed 'rough and ready' furniture that incorporated a multitude of salvaged and recycled elements. His eccentrically formed chaise-longue with woven rush is more typical of his recent work, which is intended for limited production.

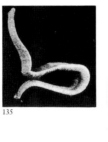

135

136

Tom Dixon, British, b. 1959

S chairs, 1988 (136)
Dixon P.I.D., UK

Bent, mild steel frames with latex rubber, rush and wicker coverings

Dixon's intriguing S chair, which is available in various tactile coverings, has a sensuous and anthropomorphic form. Aggressive curves define what appear to be the narrow waist and full hips of the chair; strangely inviting, its bent cantilevered shape allows a comfortable, springy action while sitting in it. Like his chaise-longue, the variations of this design are intended for limited production; the rubber S chair illustrated is a prototype and this version is not available.

Fred Baier, British, b. 1949

Desk, 1989
Fred Baier, UK

137

Applied metallic finish on birch plywood construction with steel sleaves and leather-covered drop leaf

Fred Baier approaches design in the manner of the Craft Revival, creating furniture with a high degree of craftsmanship, yet designates function the lowest priority. His extraordinarily formed, brightly coloured, anti-craft-design constructions, such as this Roll Top Drop Leaf Transforming Robot Desk of 1989, with Japanese sci-fi kitsch references, suggest the unexpected existence of an underlying subversive tendency in the Craft Revival.

Mark Robson, British, b. 1965

GRP chairs, 1989 (138)
Fiell, UK

Moulded GRP (glass-reinforced polyester) with a cellulose finish

138

Mark Robson graduated from the Royal College of Art in 1989. The vigorous asymmetry of his three-legged GRP chair underlines his interest in pushing materials to their limits. With function strongly considered, Robson has taken advantage of the plasticity of GRP and allowed its full potential to be realized in a fluid, organic shape. Apparently granting the medium a life of its own, the GRP chair literally grew around Robson as he constructed it while assuming different sitting positions within it.

Elisabeth Garouste, French, b. 1949 and **Mattia Bonetti**, French (born in Italy), b. 1953

Star sofa, c. 1988 (139)
Neotu, France

139

Cotton velvet-covered foam upholstery on wooden frame with gilded bronze legs

Elisabeth Garouste and Mattia Bonetti studied at the École Camondo and the Centro Scolastico per l'Industria Artistica respectively. For their first exhibition together in 1981 they produced a collection of 'primitive' objects that were inspired by ancient symbolism and mysticism. The one-off Star sofa represents a progression from these earlier designs to more formal and stylized forms.

Marco Zanuso Jr, Italian

Table, 1989 (140)
Neotu, France

Coloured and lacquered beech top and legs with nickel-plated metal supports

Marco Zanuso Jr, son of the well-known Italian designer of the same name, has produced furniture for Memphis. The I Buoni Sentimenti illustrated here is an elegant dining table that was designed with a matching wardrobe and is part of a special limited edition.

Elisabeth Garouste, French, b. 1949 and **Mattia Bonetti**, French (born in Italy), b. 1953

Imperial chair, *c.* 1988 (141)
Neotu, France

Raffia skirting on orange-painted natural wood branches

Working in reaction to the industrial process of design, Garouste and Bonetti produce limited-edition and one-off furniture, 'inspired by history and imagination', which has evolved from 'meaningful ritual, wild, ancient and enduring, expressing an indefinable contemporary yearning for mystery and poetry' (*see Avant Première*, exhibition catalogue, Victoria and Albert Museum, 1988, page 21).

Martin Szekely, French, b. 1956

Liberata table, 1989 (142)
Neotu, France

Peroba veneer on MDF with nickel-plated feet

Szekely designs high-quality furniture collections that are produced in limited editions: his success results from a positive collaboration between designer and *fabricant* (manufacturer).

Elisabeth Garouste, French, b. 1949 and **Mattia Bonetti**, French (born in Italy), b. 1953

Afrika table, 1990
Neotu, France

Solid oak with pear-wood cabochons and wrought-iron rivets

Garouste and Bonetti's tribal 'primitif' style has been called 'New Caledonie Gothique'. Their highly crafted Afrika table is part of a special limited edition.

Konstantin Grcic, German (born in Austria), b. 1965

Armchair and side chair, 1990 (144)
Fiell, UK

Solid beech construction

Grcic is able strike a sophisticated and harmonious balance of pure design and craftsmanship in his work that makes reference to the Milan and Turin schools of the late 1940s and early 1950s. Like such postwar furniture, the armchair and side chair illustrated, entitled Briol, 'exude a seriousness, precision and drastic economy that makes them less quickly understandable' (*see* C. and K. Fehrman, *Postwar Interior Design: 1945–1960*, New York 1987, page 76).

Collecting modern furniture

Furniture designed after 1945 is a relatively new field for collectors. Through various international revivals of interest in the social history of the recent past, in particular the 1950s and 1960s, it is not surprising that the classic design from these decades has created a new area of connoisseurship and is highly sought after today. In recent years, salerooms such as Sotheby's and Christie's have begun to hold auctions that include, or that are solely dedicated to, the decorative arts since 1945, and a number of reference books on the subject have been published.

As in all areas of collecting, it is essential to understand the process by which value is quantified. The determining criteria are as follows: authorship, rarity, historic importance, provenance/ documentation, sales precedents, condition, and fashion. It should be pointed out that not only do these factors take on a different order of priority according to the piece being assessed, but also that it is unwise to rely upon any given value as being 'objective'; a classic piece of design is only worth what someone else is prepared to pay for it in the current market. Although some furniture from the postwar period has substantially appreciated in value over a short period of time, collecting purely for investment is not generally to be recommended.

The availability of fine and important furniture, particularly from the late 1940s and early 1950s, is becoming increasingly limited. Italian design from the Milan and Turin schools is the most collectable and commands the highest prices: a Carlo Mollino Arabesque coffee table of laminated wood realized $50,600 at Sotheby's New York on 1 December 1990 and in 1985 a wooden and glass-topped desk, also designed by Mollino, sold at auction in Venice for $140,000, the world record price for a postwar furniture design. The dominant characteristic of most of the highly desirable furniture from this period is its rarity. Often it was commissioned or designed for specific locations – this is especially the case with much of Mollino's work – and if the proper documentation exists, then the value of the piece may be greatly enhanced.

With the large sums of money involved, collectors of this type of furniture should either be very well informed or should seek the advice of a reputable dealer or saleroom expert. Period and contemporary forgeries in this market are not unknown, nor are original variations on designs, which often complicate the verification of authenticity. Only after careful deliberation and extensive research may these latter pieces be deemed genuine.

Prototypes of mass-produced designs can in some instances, on the basis of their historical importance, be assigned a value commensurate with important one-off or site-specific furniture. Designers such as Charles Eames developed numerous prototypes that predate the related production run by a number of years. Occasionally, Eames would also refine and adapt details on a design to improve its initial performance or process of manufacture. This early developmental furniture, which led to acknowledged classic designs, is particularly rare and although most examples are in the possession of national and exceptional private collections, they do occasionally surface in the marketplace, where they represent one of the most astute investments in this field of collecting.

For most collectors of modern furniture, condition is a particularly important issue, especially if the piece is to function as originally intended. The best advice when contemplating an acquisition is to avoid those examples that require significant restoration. Always attempt to locate the design that is in the best possible condition. Intact manufacturers' labels or marks can often greatly enhance the value of a particular design: for instance, a Charles Eames LCW with an Evans Products label accurately dates the chair as having been produced between 1946 and 1949, making it more collectable than the same chair from the later Herman Miller edition. Never remove labels, whether fabric, paper or plastic, as quite often these are the only means of proving a design's authenticity.

The condition of plastic furniture is particularly critical: unlike designs constructed of wood, which often appear more attractive when slightly distressed or with signs of a natural patina, plastic surfaces look dreadful with even the mildest damage. Plastic does not age well and it is intended to possess a 'clean' finish, as though it were brand new. There is no way to revive plastic once it has perished, so it is essential to consider only those examples in very good condition.

Even within the middle range of the collectors' market, fakes are commonplace; indeed, the proliferation of cheap period copies of high style designs was one of the reasons why Herman Miller moved out of the domestic marketplace in the late 1950s. Recently, we have seen clever copies of such seminal designs as Arne Jacobsen's Egg chair and Eero Saarinen's Womb chair. From the point of view of the collector, there is no advantage at all in acquiring these early forgeries, nor is there any benefit in investing in a contemporary unlicenced version of a classic period design.

Through the rapidly increasing interest in and demand for design since 1945, prices have risen considerably, as good examples of furniture from this period become more difficult to find. Serious collectors are well advised to seek the advice and assistance of established specialist dealers who, through an international network of sources, can locate specific designs of the highest quality. The most important recommendation for collectors, however, is to buy only what you like – and to enjoy it.

Specialist dealers

Australia

Design & Decoration, 419A King Street, Newtown, Victoria 2042 (519-2258)

Belgium

Galerie Cotthem, Molenstraat 28B, 9300 Aalst (091-60-72-58)
Galerie Dewindt, 77–79 rue Lebeau, 1000 Brussels (513-36-12)

France

Galerie Neotu, 25 rue du Renard, 75004 Paris (42-78-91-83)
Galerie Yves Gastou, 12 rue Bonaparte, 75006 Paris (46-34-27-17)

Germany

Galerie Artificial, Hummelsteiner Weg 76, 8500 Nuremberg 40 (0911-33-55-75)
Galerie Ulrich Fiedler, Lindenstrasse 19, D-5000 Cologne 1 (0221-2-40-13-38)

Italy

Translucido, Via dello Sproue 1, Florence (055-212750)

The Netherlands

Rotor, Singel 105, 1012 VG Amsterdam (020-257736)

United Kingdom

Fiell, 181–183 King's Road, London SW3 (071-351-7172)
Gallery 25, 4 Halkin Arcade, Motcomb Street, London SW1 (071-235-5178)
Themes & Variations, 231 Westbourne Grove, London W11 (071-727-5531)

United States of America and Canada

Barry Friedman Ltd, 1117 Madison Avenue, New York, New York 10028 (212-794-8950)
Celebrating 20th Century Design, 341 Lafayette Street (at Bleecker), New York, New York 10012 (212-529-2724)
Double KK Gallery, 318 North La Cienaga Boulevard, Los Angeles, California 90048 (213-652-5990)
Fifty/50, 793 Broadway (10th and 11th Streets), New York, New York 10003 (212-777-3208)
Fred Silberman & Co., 83 Wooster Street, New York, New York 10012 (212-925-9470)
Free Form, 85 Eighth Avenue, New York, New York 10012 (212-924-2375)
Full House, 133 Wooster Street, New York, New York 10012 (212-529-2298)
20th Century, 23 Beverley Street, Toronto M5T 1XS (416-598-2172)
280 Modern, 280 Lafayette Street, New York, New York 10012 (212-941-5825)

Galleries and Museums

Europe

Bauhaus Collections, Ernst Ludwig Haus, Mathildenhoe, 6100 Darmstadt, Hesse, Germany
Boymans-van Beuningen Museum, Mathenesserlaan 18–20, Rotterdam, The Netherlands
Brighton Art Gallery and Museum, Royal Pavilion, Brighton BN1, UK
The British Museum, Great Russell Street, London WC1, UK
Carolino Augusteum Museum, Museumsplatz 6, A-5010 Salzburg, Austria
Centre Georges Pompidou, 75004 Paris, France
The Crafts Council, 12 Waterloo Place, London SW1, UK
Danske Kunstindustrimuseet, Bredgade 68, 1260 Copenhagen, Denmark
The Design Council, 28 Haymarket, London SW1, UK
The Design Museum, Butlers Wharf, 28 Shad Thames, London SE1, UK
The Geffrye Museum, Kingsland Road, Shoreditch, London E2, UK
Gemeentemuseum, Stadhouderslaan 41, The Hague, The Netherlands
The Hunterian Museum and Art Gallery, The University, Glasgow G12, UK
Kunstgewerbemuseum, c/o Staatliche Museen Preussischer, Kulturbesitz, 1000 Berlin 61, Germany
Kunstgewerbemuseum, Ausstellungstrasse 60, 8031 Zurich, Switzerland
Kunstmuseum, Ehrenhof 3–5, Düsseldorf, Germany
Manchester City Art Gallery, Mosley Street, Manchester M2, UK
The Montreal Museum of Decorative Arts, Château Dufresne, Montreal, Quebec, Canada
Musée d'Art Moderne, La Ville de Paris, 9 rue Gaston de Saint-Paul, 75016 Paris, France
Musée des Arts Décoratifs, 107 rue de Rivoli, 75001 Paris, France
Museum für Angewardte Kunst, Stubenring 5, A-1010 Vienna, Austria
Museum für Kunst und Gerwerbe, Steintorplatz – D-2000, Hamburg 1, Germany
Museum of Applied Art, Munich, Germany

Museum of Applied Arts, Helsinki, Finland
Museo Alchimia, Via Torino 68, 20123 Milan, Italy
Nationalmuseum, 103 24 Stockholm, Sweden
Nordenfjeldske Kunstindustrimuseum, Munkegaten 5, 7000 Trondheim, Norway
The Royal Scottish Museum, Chambers Street, Edinburgh EH1, UK
Smalands Museum, Vaxjo, Finland
Stedelijk Museum, Paulus Potterstraat 13, 5082 Amsterdam, The Netherlands
Suomen Rakennustaiteen Museum, Helsinki, Finland
Tiroler Landes-Museum Ferdinandeum, Museumstrasse 15, Innsbruck, Austria
Victoria and Albert Museum, Cromwell Road, London SW7, UK
Vitra Design Museum, 1 Charles Eames Street, 7858 Weil Am Rhein, Germany

United States of America

American Craft Museum, West 53rd Street, New York, New York 10019
The Art Institute of Chicago, Michigan Avenue at Adams Street, Chicago, Illinois 60603
The Brooklyn Museum, 200 Eastern Parkway, New York, New York 11238
Cincinatti Contemporary Arts Centre, 115 East 5th Street, Cincinatti, Ohio 45203
The Cooper-Hewitt Museum, The Smithsonian Institution's National Museum of Design, 2 East 91st Street, New York, New York 10028
The Detroit Institute of Arts, 5200 Woodward Avenue, Detroit, Michigan 48202
Grand Rapids Art Museum, 155 Division North, Grand Rapids, Michigan 49503
The Indianapolis Museum of Art, 1200 West 38th Street, Indianapolis 46208
The Metropolitan Museum of Art, Fifth Avenue at 83rd Street, New York, New York 10028
The M.I.T. Museum, 265 Massachusetts Avenue, Cambridge, Massachusetts
Museum of Fine Arts, 465 Huntington Avenue, Boston, Massachusetts 02115
The Museum of Modern Art, 11 West 53rd Street, New York, New York 10019

National Academy of Design, 1083 Fifth Avenue, New York, New York
New York Design Centre, Thompson Avenue, Long Island City, New York, New York 11101
Pennsylvania Academy of the Fine Arts, Broad and Cherry Streets, Philadelphia, Pennsylvania 19102
Philadelphia Museum of Art, Benjamin Franklin Parkway, Philadelphia, Pennsylvania 19130
Saint Louis Museum of Art, Forest Park, Saint Louis, Missouri 63110
Virginia Museum of Fine Arts, Boulevard and Grove, Richmond, Virginia 23221
The Whitney Museum of American Art, 75th Street and Madison Avenue, New York, New York 10021

Notes on the text

Introduction: Ornament in exile
(*pp. 7–15*)

1 John Neuhart, Marilyn Neuhart and Ray Eames, *Eames Design: The Work of the Office of Charles and Ray Eames*, Thames and Hudson, London 1989, p. 14
2 Isabel Anscombe and Charlotte Gere, *Arts and Crafts in Britain and America*, Academy Editions, London 1978, p. 13
3 Institute of Contemporary Arts, *The Modern Chair: Twentieth-Century British Chair Design*, ICA, London 1988, pp. 12–13
4 Derek Ostergard, *Mackintosh to Mollino: Fifty Years of Chair Design*, Barry Friedman, New York 1984, p. 13
5 Whitechapel Art Gallery, *Modern Chairs 1918–1970*, Whitechapel Art Gallery, London 1970, p. 1
6 Reyer Kras, *Gerrit Rietveld: A Centenary Exhibition*, Barry Friedman, New York 1988, p. 28
7 Lois Maassen, *Herman Miller Magazine*, Herman Miller Inc., Zeeland, Michigan 1989, p. 11
8 Frank Russell, Philippe Garner and John Read, *A Century of Chair Design*, Academy Editions, London 1980, p. 113
9 J. Stewart Johnson, *Alvar Aalto: Furniture and Glass*, The Museum of Modern Art, New York 1984, p. 6
10 Kathryn Hiesinger and George Marcus, *Design Since 1945*, Thames and Hudson, London 1983, p. 221
11 Whitney Museum of American Art, *High Styles: Twentieth-Century American Design*, Summit Books, New York 1985, p. 137

1 Reconstruction and rationalism
(*pp. 16–24*)

1 *High Styles*, p. 132
2 Marian Page, *Furniture Designed by Architects*, Whitney Library of Design, New York 1980, p. 208
3 Cherie Fehrman and Kenneth Fehrman, *Postwar Interior Design: 1945–1960*, Van Nostrand Company Inc., New York 1987, p. 23
4 Ralph Caplan, *The Design of Herman Miller*, Whitney Library of Design, New York 1976, p. 32

5   George Nelson and Henry Wright, *Tomorrow's House: A Complete Guide for the Home Builder*, Simon & Schuster, New York 1946, p. 19
6   Fehrman and Fehrman, p. 18
7   The Detroit Institute of Arts and The Metropolitan Museum of Art, *Design in America: The Cranbrook Vision 1925–1950*, Harry N. Abrams, New York 1983, p. 142
8   Fehrman and Fehrman, p. 24
9   Ibid.
10   Neuhart, Neuhart and Eames, p. 27
11   Penny Sparke, *Italian Design: 1870 to the Present*, Thames and Hudson, London 1988, p. 80
12   Hiesinger and Marcus, p. 223

2   **The ascendancy of organic design**
    (pp. 48–56)

1   Nicholas Drake, *The fifties in Vogue*, Condé Nast Publications, London 1987, p. 6
2   Whitechapel Art Gallery, *Modern Chairs 1918–1970*, Whitechapel Art Gallery, London 1970, p. 29
3   Eric Larrabee and Massimo Vignelli, *Knoll Design*, Harry N. Abrams, New York 1981, p. 6
4   The New Furniture Group, press release, Laverne International, New York, 4 June 1953
5   *Modern Chairs 1918–1970*, p. 30
6   Fehrman and Fehrman, p. 25
7   Deyan Sudjic, *From Matt Black to Memphis and Back Again*, Architecture Design & Technology Press, London 1989, p. 99
8   Ibid.
9   Albrecht Bangert, *Italian Furniture Design: Ideas Styles Movements*, Bangert Verlag/Bangert Publications, Munich 1988, p. 33
10   Fehrman and Fehrman, p. 76
11   Bangert, p. 16
12   Centrokappa, *Il Design Italiano Degli Anni'50*, R.D.E., Milan 1985, p. 304
13   Ibid.
14   Virgilio Vercelloni, *The Adventure of Design: Gavina*, Editoriale Jaca Book spa, Milan 1987, p. 15
15   Ann Lee Morgan, *Contemporary Designers*, St James Press, London 1985, p. 471
16   Richard Hamilton, *Collected Words 1953–1982*, Thames and Hudson, London 1982, pp. 148–49

3   **Pop culture and anti-design**
    (pp. 80–88)

1   Penny Sparke, *The Plastics Age: From Modernity to Post-Modernity*, Victoria and Albert Museum, London 1990, p. 93
2   Abraham Moles, 'Functionalism in Crisis', *Ulm*, August 1967, p. 24
3   Sutherland Lyall, *Hille: 75 Years of British Furniture*, Elron Press/Victoria and Albert Museum, London 1981, p. 49
4   Nigel Whiteley, *Pop Design: Moderism to Mod*, The Design Council, London 1987, p. 88
5   Hamilton, p. 28
6   Whiteley, p. 138
7   Hiesinger and Marcus, p. xix
8   Jennifer Harris, Sarah Hyde and Greg Smith, *1966 and All That: Design and Consumerism in Britain 1960–1969*, Trefoil Books, London 1986, p. 25
9   Hiesinger and Marcus, p. 19
10   Morgan, p. 382
11   Ignazia Favata, *Joe Colombo and Italian Design of the Sixties*, Thames and Hudson, London 1988, p. 6
12   Andrea Branzi, *The Hot House; Italian New Wave Design*, Thames and Hudson, London 1984, pp. 73–74
13   Giuliana Gramigna, *Repertory 1950–1980*, Arnoldo Mondadori Editore, Milan 1985, p. 147
14   Branzi, p. 6
15   Hiesinger and Marcus, p. 25
16   Whiteley, p. 125

4   **Conformist, reformist or contesting**
    (pp. 112–20)

1   *The Modern Chair*, p. 44
2   Branzi, pp. 80–81
3   Bangert, p. 61
4   Branzi, p. 127
5   Michael Collins and Andreas Papadakis, *Post-Modern Design*, Academy Editions, London 1989, p. 28
6   Branzi, p. 49
7   Michael Collins, *Towards Post-Modernism: Design Since 1851*, British Museum Publications, London 1987, p. 117
8   Collins and Papadakis, p. 28
9   Ibid.
10   Ibid.

5   **The eclectic years**
    (pp. 144–52)

1   Peter Dormer, *The New Furniture: Trends and Traditions*, Thames and Hudson, London and New York 1987, p. 136
2   Sparke 1988, p. 186
3   Sparke 1988, pp. 217–18
4   Branzi, p. 49
5   Penny Sparke, *Furniture: Twentieth-Century Design*, E.P. Dutton, New York 1986, p. 99
6   Sudjic, *From Matt Black to Memphis*, p. 202
7   Deyan Sudjic, *Ron Arad: Restless Furniture*, Fourth Estate/Wordsearch, London 1989, p. 1
8   Sudjic, *Ron Arad*, p. 17
9   *The Modern Chair*, p. 51

Biographies

Throughout the book, designers' dates have been provided wherever possible

Eero Aarnio, Finnish, b. 1932
Trained at the Helsinki University of Industrial Arts from 1954 to 1957. In 1962, he opened his own design office, working primarily as an interior and industrial designer. He came to prominence in the 1960s with a series of fibreglass chairs, including the Globe and the Pastille, winning an A.I.D. award for the latter in 1968.

Franco Albini, Italian, 1905–77
Originally from Lake Como, Albini trained in architecture at the Politecnico di Milano, graduating in 1929. He exhibited at the Monza Biennale as a rationalist in the 1930s and was the greatest champion of rationalism in Italy during the immediate postwar years. He was editor of *Casabella* from 1945 to 1946. From 1951 until his death he co-designed furniture with his associate, Franca Helg.

Ron Arad, British (born in Israel), b. 1951
Studied at the Jerusalem Academy of Art (1971–73) and later at the Architectural Association in London, graduating in 1979. In 1981, he established his own design practice, One Off Ltd. Working mainly as a furniture designer, Arad has also completed several interior design briefs, including the Tel Aviv Opera House (1990). Arad's work is skilfully constructed and is meant to have permanence. Often monumental in size, his furniture designs are highly sculptural yet eminently comfortable.

Gae(tana) Aulenti, Italian, b. 1927
Trained in architecture at the Politecnico di Milano (graduating in 1954), where she has been a faculty member since 1964. During the 1950s, she worked within the Neo-Liberty style, which was opposed to mainstream rationalism. Primarily recognized for her designs for lighting, Aulenti has also designed furniture for Kartell, Poltronova, Knoll International and Zanotta. She has worked extensively as an interior designer throughout her career and since 1975 has collaborated with the Italian theatre director Luca Ronconi, designing stage sets.

Fred Baier, British, b. 1949
Studied furniture design at Birmingham College of Art (1969–72) and later at the Royal College of Art, London (1973–76). In 1971 he was awarded a bursary by the Royal Society of Arts and in 1976 received the Crafts Advisory Committee's major award. He has taught at Brighton Polytechnic (1979–82), the Wendell Castle School, based in New York State (1976–78) and currently lectures at the Royal College of Art. His work has been exhibited throughout Europe and America and in 1990 he showed several of his designs at the Crafts Council, London.

Mario Bellini, Italian, b. 1935
Trained in architecture at the Politecnico di Milano, graduating in 1959. He has worked as a design consultant for, among others, Cassina, Olivetti, C & B Italia, Macatre, Brion-Vega, Renault and Fiat. His furniture designs, such as the Cab chair, are innovative in form yet intended for rational methods of production. He received Compasso d'Oro awards in 1962, 1964, 1970 and 1979. He has his own architectural practice based in Milan and is an editor of *Domus*.

Harry Bertoia, American (born in Italy), 1915–78
Trained at the Cranbrook Academy of Art, Michigan, from 1937 to 1939. Having established the Cranbrook metalworking studio he directed that department between 1939 and 1943, becoming a faculty member. During the Second World War, Bertoia worked with Charles and Ray Eames at Evans Products Company developing advanced techniques for moulding plywood and in the late 1940s he continued to work with the Eameses at the Plyformed Products Company in Venice, California. His series of wire rod chairs designed for Knoll International were so commercially successful that they enabled Bertoia to pursue a career as a sculptor.

Mattia Bonetti, French (born in Italy), b. 1953
Studied at the Centro Scolastico per l'Industria Artistica, where he became interested in textile design. He moved to Paris and became a colour consultant to Rhone-Pollenc and a stylist working with Marie Berani before collaborating with the architect Andrée Putman. In the early 1980s he formed a collaboration with Elisabeth Garouste, designing limited-production and one-off pieces of furniture.

Osvaldo Borsani, Italian, b. 1911
Osvaldo and Fulgenzio Borsani's company, Tecno, evolved from their father's workshop known as Atelier Varedo and the later small firm Arredamento Borsani. Osvaldo was the primary designer for Tecno in the 1950s; only a few pieces by other designers were manufactured. Tecno's product line was the direct result of a commitment to technological research and development rather than spontaneous creativity.

Andrea Branzi, Italian, b. 1938
Studied architecture in Florence, graduating in 1966. In the same year he became a founding member of Archizoom Associati. Throughout the late 1960s and 1970s Branzi was one of the primary exponents of Radical design. In 1977 he organized with Michele De Lucchi the first major retrospective exhibition of Italian postwar design. He was a founding member of Studio Alchymia and in the early 1980s contributed to the work of Memphis. Branzi is the educational director at the Domus Academy, Milan, which was established in 1982 as a postgraduate college for the teaching of 'New Design'.

Achille Castiglioni, Italian, b. 1918
Based in Como, Achille has worked from 1944 in collaboration with his brothers, Pier Giacomo and Livio (all trained at the Politecnico di Milano). They are primarily known for their lighting designs, however, Achille and Pier Giacomo were the first designers to explore the idea of 'readymade' furniture. In 1957, the brothers held an exhibition at the baroque Olmo Villa in Lake Como, entitled 'Forme e Colori nella Casa D'Oggi', which incorporated their readymade designs. With this exhibition they were able to challenge existing concepts in interior design. Achille's furniture, such as the Primate kneeling stool of

1970, is highly innovative in both form and function. He has received seven Compasso d'Oro awards and was instrumental in the founding of the Italian A.D.I. awards.

Wendell Castle, American, b. 1932
Studied sculpture at the University of Kansas, graduating with an MA in 1961. He is the most celebrated American advocate of the Craft Revival and is best known for his virtuoso work in wood, although in the late 1960s he experimented briefly with fibreglass, producing the surreal Molar and Castle series. His furniture designs from the late 1970s and 1980s are exceptionally well crafted and often utilize *trompe l'oeil* effects.

Franco Cavatorta, Italian, b. 1925
The Cavatorta family workshop was founded in Rome by Eugenio Cavatorta in 1888 to produce high-quality, exclusive furniture. Franco Cavatorta studied with Finn Juhl and Arne Jacobsen, who undoubtedly influenced his approach to furniture design; he also collaborated on a number of projects with Mario De Renzi and Giorgio Quaroni in the 1950s and more recently has worked with Robert Venturi.

Joe Colombo, Italian, 1930–71
Studied at the Accademia di Belle Arti (Brera Academy), Milan, before training in architecture at the Politecnico di Milano. From 1951 to 1955 he worked as an independent painter and sculptor; in the 1950s he also formed the Nuclear Painting Movement and in 1955 became a founding member of the Art Concret Group. He established his own design studio in 1962. Throughout his short yet highly prolific career, he designed furniture, lighting products and micro-environments for, among others, Kartell, Comfort, Flexiform, O-Luce and Bayer. His work was always highly futuristic and was founded on an optimistic belief in advanced technology. He was profoundly interested in the Orient and shortly before his untimely death wrote, in collaboration with Pierre Paulin and Sori Yanagi, *New Form Furniture: Japan* (published in 1970).

Robin Day, British, b. 1915
Studied at the Royal College of Art in London, graduating in 1939. In 1948, he and Clive Latimer won first prize for a storage concept exhibited at the 'International Competition for Low-Cost Furniture Design', Museum of Modern Art, New York. The international acclaim Day received with these prizewinning designs brought him to the attention of the furniture manufacturer, Hille: a year later, the company appointed him their design director. His greatest commercial success was the Polypropylene chair of 1963 – the first truly low-cost, multi-purpose plastic chair designed for mass production.

Michele De Lucchi, Italian, b. 1951
Studied in Padua and later studied architecture at the Università degli Studi, Florence, from which he graduated in 1975. While there he founded the Cavart group. In 1977, he collaborated with Andrea Branzi and organized the first major retrospective exhibition of Italian postwar design, 'Italian Design of the Fifties', staged just outside Milan. He designed for Studio Alchymia and later for Memphis. In 1979 he became a design consultant for Olivetti Synthesis, Massa and in 1984 he transferred to Olivetti, Ivrea and worked on several projects with Ettore Sottsass. He has worked for Sottsass Associates and has designed products and furniture for a number of manufacturers.

Tom Dixon, British, b. 1959
A self-taught metal-worker based in London, Dixon operates his own workshop and produces one-off and limited-production furniture. His work is highly expressive and often makes use of 'found' objects. He has exhibited his designs internationally and they have been especially well received in Japan.

Charles Eames, American, 1907–78
Studied architecture at Saint Louis University and in 1936 received a fellowship at the Cranbrook Academy of Art, Michigan where he later taught. During the Second World War, with his wife Ray (née Kaiser), Eames was commissioned by the U.S. Navy to produce plywood splints and litters. For this project they developed a method of moulding laminated wood into three-dimensional compound curves. Eames collaborated with Eero Saarinen on a series of plywood chairs, which made use of this new technique, for the Museum of Modern Art's 'Organic Design in Home Furnishings' competition of 1940. At this exhibition, they won two first prizes and in 1946, Charles Eames was given the Museum's first one-man show. In 1948, Eames won second prize at the Museum's 'International Competition for Low-Cost Furniture Design' with his proposal for a moulded fibreglass chair, which later became the first plastic mass-produced piece of furniture. Eames worked closely with the manufacturer Herman Miller, creating highly innovative, rational furniture design throughout the 1950s and 1960s. It should be noted that Ray Eames was very often involved in the design of pieces that are attributed solely to Charles Eames.

Piero Fornasetti, Italian, 1913–88
Studied fine art at the Liceo Artistico, Milan and later at the Accademia di Belle Arti (Brera Academy), Milan. In the late 1930s he met Gio Ponti, with whom he subsequently formed a collaboration. Together they designed many interiors, including the San Remo Casino. Fornasetti established his own shop in Milan and produced numerous designs for furniture, textiles, glass and ceramics. His highly decorative furniture designs were expensive and time-consuming to produce and therefore ran counter to the rationalism that prevailed in the work of other designers; indeed, he can be seen as the great anomaly of postwar Italian design, for he broadly rejected modernism and promoted anti-design, at a time when many of his contemporaries were conforming to a kind of design 'morality'.

Elisabeth Garouste, French, b. 1949
Studied at the École Camondo and the Charpentier workshop. Initially she designed stage sets and theatrical costumes. In the early 1980s she met Mattia Bonetti and formed a collaboration with him designing interiors, including a Paris salon for Christian Lacroix, Hachette's office interiors on the Boulevard Saint-Michel, the 'Fakes' exhibition staged at Fondation Cartier in Jouy-en-Josas and furniture for the Parisian gallery, Neotu.

Frank Gehry, American (born in Canada), b. 1929
Studied architecture at the

University of Southern California in Los Angeles and later graduated from Harvard University, Massachusetts. He established his own design office in 1962. Primarily known for his architectural work, Gehry designed two series of cardboard furniture, entitled Easy Edges and Experimental Edges, in 1972 and between 1980 and 1985 respectively. Gehry later designed the Vitra Design Museum, Weil Am Rhein, Germany, which houses an extensive collection of furniture from the immediate postwar years to the present day.

Michael Graves, American, b. 1934
Trained in architecture at Harvard and since 1962 has taught at Princeton University in New Jersey. Primarily working as an architect, Graves designed furniture for Memphis in the 1980s. His use of applied classical motifs has led him to become known as a 'post-modern classicist'.

Robert Heritage, British, b. 1927
Trained at the Royal College of Art in London and subsequently opened his own design office in 1953. He designed several sideboards that were manufactured by A.G. Evans, Archie Shine and Race Furniture Ltd.

Hans Hollein, Austrian, b. 1934
Trained at the Federal Technical College of Graphic Arts in Vienna, graduating in 1956. Later he studied at Illinois Institute of Technology, Chicago and the University of California. In 1964, he established his own design office based in Vienna. One of the most accomplished post-modern architects and designers, he has designed furniture and products for Poltronova, Memphis and Alessi.

Arne Jacobsen, Danish, 1902–71
Studied architecture at the Royal Danish Academy of Fine Arts, Copenhagen, graduating in 1928. A leading figure in Scandinavian design, he exploited the potential offered by new technology and mass production while remaining consistently truthful to the materials he employed. The Ant chair (1951), the Egg chair (1957) and the graceful Swan chair (1959) are highly innovative in form and they also predict the more literal interpretation of organic design that was to prevail during the decade that followed.

Finn Juhl, Danish, b. 1912
Studied architecture under Kaare Klint while at the Royal Danish Academy of Fine Arts, Copenhagen. In 1937, he formed a collaboration with Niels Vodder, a cabinet-maker who handcrafted Juhl's designs. During the 1950s, Juhl's less exclusive furniture was mass-produced in America by Barker.

Vladimir Kagan, American (born in Germany), b. 1928
Studied architecture at Columbia University and learnt cabinet-making skills in his father's workshop. From the late 1940s he has designed furniture which he has shown at the Museum of Modern Art and the Cooper-Hewitt Museum, New York. Throughout his career he has received many prestigious contracts, including those from the General Electric Company, Monsanto, the Prudential Insurance Company, Warner Communications, American Express and Walt Disney Enterprises. He was honoured with a thirty-year retrospective exhibition of his work at the Fashion Institute of Technology, New York. He has received numerous awards and recognition for his innovative designs and is currently President of the New York Metropolitan Chapter of the A.S.I.D.

Rodney Kinsman, British, b. 1943
Studied furniture design at the Central School of Art and in 1966 established a design consultancy partnership, OMK, based in London. He is a strict rationalist and is best known for his Omkstak chair of 1971, a design that epitomizes the High-Tech style of the 1970s.

Toshiyuki Kita, Japanese, b. 1942
Studied industrial design at the University for Design, Osaka, graduating in 1964. In the same year, he established his own design office based in Osaka, but since 1969 has divided his time between Japan and Italy. He has collaborated on design projects with Silvio Coppola, Giotto Stoppino and Bepi Fiori. He has received many awards for his work including the Japanese Interior Design Award (1975).

Poul Kjaerholm, Danish, b. 1929
Studied design at the School of Arts and Crafts in Copenhagen (graduating in 1952), where he also taught between 1952 and 1956. He has worked as a freelance designer, creating furniture for Fritz Hansen and E. Kolb Christensen. His work, such as the PK24 chaise, results from a profound understanding of the International Style – especially the work of Mies van der Rohe – and is often suffused with the Scandinavian love of natural materials.

Florence Knoll, American, b. 1917
Graduated from the Architectural Association, London, before working in the Massachusetts-based architectural practice of Walter Gropius and Marcel Breuer. Later she worked with Hans Knoll, whom she married in 1946. In the same year they founded Knoll Associates Inc., which designed, manufactured and retailed furniture as well as undertaking interior design briefs. After her husband's untimely death in 1955 she continued to design furniture and interiors, bringing Knoll worldwide acclaim.

Shiro Kuramata, Japanese, 1934–91
Studied cabinet-making before establishing his own design practice in 1965. During the early 1980s he created designs for Memphis. He was primarily recognized for his work in interior design and designed shops for Seibu and Issey Miyake. In recognition of his work, he was awarded the Japanese Cultural Design Prize in 1981.

Danny Lane, British (born in America), b. 1955
Lane emigrated to Britain in 1975 and initially worked with Patrick Reyntiens, a craftsman in stained glass. He later studied painting at the Central School of Art, London, graduating in 1980. In 1981, he established a studio in London's East End and his own company, Glassworks, two years later. In 1984 he began a three-year association with Ron Arad and the One Off showroom. He produces mainly limited-edition furniture and sculpture and exhibits extensively abroad.

Estelle and **Erwine Laverne**, American, b. 1915 and 1909
Studied painting under Hans Hoffmann at the Art Students' League, New York (as did Ray Eames). In 1938 they founded their own company, Laverne Originals, which produced furniture and textiles designed by themselves and

others. In 1957 the Invisible Group of chairs was launched and the Lavernes then licenced the techniques of using plexiglass to other manufacturers. Laverne furniture was extremely popular with interior designers in the late 1950s and predicted the direction furniture design would take in the 1960s.

Raymond Loewy, American (born in France), 1893–1986
Studied engineering in France before working as a graphic and set designer in New York. In 1930, Loewy founded his own design office and subsequently worked in all areas of design. He was so prolific that it has been reckoned that during the 1940s and 1950s, three-quarters of the American population came into daily contact with one of his products or designs. One of the most celebrated designers of our time, Loewy was highly instrumental in raising the status of designers within industry.

Vico Magistretti, Italian, b. 1920
Trained in architecture at the Politecnico di Milano, graduating in 1945. Throughout his highly successful career his furniture has always been rationally conceived, truthful to materials and supremely elegant. He has twice been awarded the Compasso d'Oro (1967 and 1969) and was highly instrumental in elevating the status of plastics within the furniture industry. He now divides his time between Milan and London, where he lectures at the Royal College of Art.

John Makepeace, British, b. 1939
Studied at Denstone College, Staffordshire and later trained in cabinet-making at a small workshop. Makepeace founded the Parnham Trust and the world-famous School for Craftsmen in Wood at Parnham House in Dorset and is the primary advocate of the Craft Revival in Britain. He believes that the industrial process of manufacturing produces furniture that is bland and uninteresting and that it deprives consumers of natural surfaces.

Alessandro Mendini, Italian, b. 1931
Mendini worked with Nizzoli Associates until 1970 and in 1973 became a founding member of Global Tools, a school of counter design and architecture. He later became one of the leading designers

for Studio Alchymia. He has written extensively on design and was editor of *Casabella* from 1970 to 1976, replacing Gio Ponti as editor of *Domus* in 1979. In 1979 he was also awarded a Compasso d'Oro.

Carlo Mollino, Italian, 1905–73
Studied architecture at the Università di Torino, graduating in 1931. His eccentric furniture designs ran counter to the prevailing rationalism of the Milanese School and have had an enduring influence on subsequent generations of anti-rational designers. His use of simple technology to create exclusive, complicated, often zoomorphically inspired furniture, has led his work to become highly sought after by collectors in recent years.

Olivier Mourgue, French, b. 1939
Studied interior design at the École Boulle (1954–58) and at the École Nationale Supérieure des Arts Décoratifs in Paris (1958–60). From 1958 to 1961 he also trained in Sweden and Finland. He began designing furniture for Airborne in 1963 and in 1965 won an A.I.D. award for his futuristic Djinn series. In 1976, he moved to Brittany from Paris and began teaching at the École d'Art, Brest.

Peter Murdoch, British, b. 1940
Studied at the Royal College of Art, London, graduating in 1963. While there he designed his Child's chair made from paperboard, which was subsequently manufactured in America. Later, in 1968, again using the same material, he designed the Those Things series. He established his own design office in 1969.

George Nelson, American, 1907–86
George Nelson was born in Hartford, Connecticut and studied architecture at Yale University, New Haven (1928–31). In 1932 he was awarded the Prix de Rome for architecture while on a fellowship at the American Academy, Rome. In 1935 he wrote several forward-thinking articles on modern architects, including one on Le Corbusier in *Pencil Points* magazine. From 1935 until 1944, he was the editor of *Architectural Forum* and from 1944 to 1949 worked as a consultant to the journal. With William Hanby he set up his first New York-based architectural practice in 1936, a partnership that lasted until 1941. In 1944, Nelson co-designed with Henry Wright a

wall storage unit that also functioned as a room divider. This novel storage concept came to the attention of the chairman of Herman Miller, D.J. De Pree, through an article in *Architectural Forum* and led to Nelson's appointment as design director of Herman Miller in 1946. In this capacity he encouraged Charles and Ray Eames to design furniture for Herman Miller. In 1947, he formed an architectural partnership with Gordon Chadwick and began designing industrial products. Nelson continued, however, to design furniture for Herman Miller, including the Basic storage components (1946), the Comprehensive storage system (1958) and the Action Office system (1964).

Isamu Noguchi, American, 1904–88
Born in Los Angeles, the son of a Japanese poet, Noguchi spent his childhood in Japan, returning to America when he was fourteen. From 1927 to 1928 he studied sculpture under Constantin Brancusi in Paris (as did Henry Moore). Although best known for his organic sculpture, Noguchi designed several tables, including the IN50 (c. 1946) which was manufactured by Herman Miller. Over a period of some thirty years Noguchi designed a large number of *akari*, or light sculptures, which were manufactured in Japan using traditional mulberry-bark paper.

Verner Panton, Danish, b. 1926
Studied at the Royal Danish Academy of Fine Arts, Copenhagen and later worked in the architectural practice of Arne Jacobsen. In 1955, he established his own design office and in 1960 developed the innovative Stacking chair, which was the first single injection-moulded, all-plastic chair and was manufactured by Herman Miller. Panton's belief in advanced technology has led him to experiment with novel furniture typologies and forms. He now lives in Switzerland.

Pierre Paulin, French, b. 1927
Studied at the École Camondo. He began designing for Thonet in 1954 and Artifort from 1958. He worked in association with Mobilier National and in 1968 participated in the refurbishment of the Louvre. In 1969, Paulin received an A.I.D.

award for his Ribbon chair (1965). A year later he designed seating for Expo '70, Osaka and in 1971 he was selected to redesign the private apartments of the Elysée Palace. In 1975, he established ADSA + Partners (where he was joined by Roger Tallon and Michael Schreiber in 1984). In 1983, Paulin was commissioned to design furniture for the presidential office at the Elysée Palace.

Gaetano Pesce, Italian, b. 1939
Trained in architecture at the Università di Venezia (1959–65) and also studied at the Institute of Industrial Design in Venice between 1961 and 1965. He has worked as an artist, film-maker and freelance designer. His Up Series (1969) designed for B & B Italia and his Sit Down series (1975) designed for Cassina were both revolutionary in their methods of production.

Warren Platner, American, b. 1919
Studied architecture at Cornell University, Ithaca, New York, graduating in 1941. He worked in the design office of Raymond Loewy and the architectural practices of I.M. Pei and Kevin Roche & John Dinkeloo. He was an associate architect at Eero Saarinen & Associates from 1950 to 1965, after which he opened his own architectural firm, Platner Associates. Since then he has worked on numerous architectural and interior design commissions, including Windows on the World, the restaurant on top of the World Trade Center, New York. He received worldwide recognition for the classic furniture designs that made up his Warren Platner Collection, which is still manufactured by Knoll International.

Gio Ponti, Italian, 1891–1979
Trained in architecture at the Politecnico di Milano, graduating in 1921. Initially he designed ceramics for Richard Ginori and in the 1920s also practised architecture. In 1928, he founded the design journal *Domus* and became one of the major advocates of Anti-Rationalism in Italy during the postwar years. From 1925 to 1979, he was director of the Monza Biennale, which later became the Milan Triennale. He taught at the Politecnico di Milano from 1936 to 1961 and collaborated with Piero

Fornasetti on numerous projects for furniture and interior design.

Ernest Race, British, 1913–64
Trained in interior design at the Bartlett School of Architecture, University of London, graduating in 1935. In 1945, he established Race Furniture and in the same year he designed his BA chair, which was the first British mass-produced furniture design: over 250,000 were made from resmelted aluminium. In 1951, he designed the Antelope chair, the Gazelle bench and the Springbok chair for use on the outside spaces of the Royal Festival Hall for the duration of the Festival of Britain. From 1954 until his death in 1964 Race worked as a freelance designer.

Gordon Russell, British, 1892–1980
Russell received no formal training in design and acquired his skills through managing a workshop that repaired period furniture. In 1927, he established Russell Workshops Ltd and two years later founded Gordon Russell Ltd. In 1940, he was selected as Royal Designer for Industry and from 1943 to 1947 he was Chairman of the Board of Trade design panel. Russell was a founding member of the Council of Industrial Design, formed in 1944 and in 1947 became its director. He taught at the Royal College of Art in London, from which he received an Honorary Doctorate shortly before his death in 1980.

Eero Saarinen, American (born in Finland), 1910–61
Son of the Finnish architect, Eliel Saarinen and the sculptor Louise (Loja) Gesellius Saarinen, Eero emigrated to America with his parents in 1923. From 1929 to 1930, he trained as a sculptor at the Academie de la Grande Chaumière, Paris and later studied architecture at Yale, graduating in 1934. He was awarded the Charles O. Matcham Fellowship, which enabled him to travel in Europe from 1934 to 1935. He met Charles Eames while teaching at the Cranbrook Academy and in 1940 they collaborated on a series of furniture designs for the Museum of Modern Art's 1940 'Organic Design in Home Furnishings' competition, for which they won two first prizes. As a result of his quest for visual and material unity in design, Saarinen created the Womb chair in 1946 and the

Pedestal Group between 1956 and 1957. From 1936 until his death, Saarinen practised architecture using free-flowing forms. His projects included the gateway arch of the Jefferson National Expansion Memorial, Saint Louis (1964), the terminal building at Dulles International Airport, Washington State and the Trans World Airlines Terminal, John F. Kennedy Airport, New York (1962).

Richard Sapper, Italian (born in Germany), b. 1932
Trained in engineering and economics at the University of Munich. Initially, Sapper designed for Daimler-Benz before moving to Italy in 1958. He worked in the office of Gio Ponti, then the design department of La Rinascente before forming a collaboration with Marco Zanuso. Together they designed several pieces of furniture, including the Child's chair (1964) and the Tizio lamp (1972). In 1968, he helped organize an exhibition of advanced technology at the Milan Triennale. From 1972, he worked with Gae Aulenti on a project for new systems of urban transport, which was eventually shown as an exhibition at the 1979 Milan Triennale. In 1980, he became the industrial design consultant for IBM.

Fred Scott, British, b. 1942
Worked as an apprentice cabinet-maker in High Wycombe, Buckinghamshire, England before winning a scholarship to the Royal College of Art in London in 1963. He was also awarded an Advanced Studies Travelling Scholarship to Scandinavia. In 1969 he started working as a freelance designer to Hille and since then he has produced several remarkable furniture designs for the company, including the Supporto (1979), the Elephant (1972) and the Orchid (1974). He now lectures at the Royal College of Art, London.

Peter Shire, American, b. 1947
Studied ceramics at the Chouinard Institute of Art. In 1972, he established his own studio and in 1975 he had his first one-man show in a Hollywood gallery. His colourful and exuberant work attracted the attention of Ettore Sottsass and he subsequently designed a number of pieces of furniture for Memphis.

Borek Sipek, Czech, b. 1949
Studied furniture design in Prague, architecture in Hamburg and philosophy at Stuttgart University. With a studio in Amsterdam, Sipek also produces designs for Sawaya & Moroni, Driade, Vitra, Cleto Munari and Alterego. He first received international acclaim with a series of limited-edition glass designs which echoed the work of Memphis. He continues to produce exclusive objects primarily in Bohemian crystal and has designed tableware in various metals. Since 1990 he has been a Professor at the Academy of Arts in Prague.

Ettore Sottsass Jr, Italian (born in Austria), b. 1917
Studied architecture at the Politecnico di Torino, graduating in 1939. In 1945, he worked with the Giuseppe Pagano group of architects and a year later began working as a freelance designer. In 1947, he established his own design office. He spent a year in America working for George Nelson Associates (1956). In the late 1950s and 1960s he designed office furniture and equipment, including his famous Valentine typewriter (1969), for Olivetti. During the 1960s, he produced several 'anti-design' pieces of furniture that were manufactured by Poltronova. In the 1970s, Sottsass was a member of Global Tools and later designed for Studio Alchymia. He was the designer central to Memphis in the 1980s, becoming the principal executant of post-modernism in the decorative arts. He has won the Compasso d'Oro several times.

Philippe Starck, French, b. 1949
Studied at the École Camondo. Initially he designed several pieces of inflatable furniture, sponsored by L. Ventura and later by Quasar. He went on to become art director of the Pierre Cardin studio, where he produced sixty-five furniture designs. In 1965, Starck won the La Vilette furniture competition and began working in product design. In 1980, he established his own manufacturing company, Starck Products. After completing several interior design commissions including the Café Costes, Starck was selected in 1983 to design the refurbishment of President Mitterrand's private apartments at the Elysée Palace. Starck became the most celebrated designer of the 1980s and has also received a number of architectual commissions, including the Naninani building, Tokyo (1987).

Martin Szekely, French, b. 1956
Having attended the École Boulle, Szekely was awarded a state scholarship to study furniture design in Italy (1984) and Japan (1985). He subsequently received a number of prestigious commissions, was made Designer of the Year in 1986 and won first prize from the V.I.A. (Valorisation de l'Innovation dans l'Ameublement) in 1987.

Floris Van den Broecke, British (born in The Netherlands), b. 1945
Studied fine art at the Arnhem Academy, The Netherlands, before training in furniture design at the Royal College of Art, London. Van den Broecke founded a partnership with Jane Dillon and Peter Wheeler in 1969. At present he is Professor of Furniture Design at the Royal College of Art.

Robert Venturi, American, b. 1925
Trained in architecture at Princeton University, graduating in 1950. He worked for Eero Saarinen & Associates, before receiving the Rome Prize Fellowship which enabled him to study from 1954 to 1956 at the American Academy, Rome. From 1957 to 1965, he taught architecture at the University of Pennsylvania and later he became Professor of Architecture at Yale. In 1964, he established his own architectural practice in Philadelphia. His first book, entitled *Complexity and Contradiction* (1966), promoted eclecticism in architecture. He later wrote *Learning from Las Vegas* (1972), which was co-written with his wife, Denise Scott-Brown, and Stephen Izenour and can be seen as a treatise on post-modernism. In 1984, he designed a collection of furniture for Knoll International which was inspired by historicism; Venturi can be seen as a typical post-modernist in that he employs exuberant colour and decoration together with reinterpretations of period decorative styles.

Hans Wegner, Danish, b. 1914
Studied at the Danish Institute of Technology, Copenhagen (1936) and later trained in cabinet-making under O. Moelgaard Nielsen at the School of Arts and Crafts, Copenhagen (1937–38). He worked initially as a furniture designer in the architectural offices of Arne Jacobsen and Erik Moller (1938–42). From 1940 until 1960 he collaborated with the cabinet-maker Johannes Hansen. He also designed for, among others, Fritz Hansen, Carl Hansen and Co. and Knoll International. In 1959 he was made an Honorary Royal Designer for Industry by the Royal Society of Arts, London.

Tappio Wirkkala, Finnish, b. 1915
Studied at the School of Industrial Arts, Helsinki (graduating in 1936), to which he was later appointed art director (1951–54). He took part in the Finnish exhibition at the 1951 Milan Triennale. Primarily recognized for his glass designs, Wirkkala produced several furniture designs in the 1950s using laminated wood which, although mass-produced, alluded to handcrafted work. An exponent of organic modernism, in 1955 he established the Wirkkala Design Studio, based in Helsinki.

Sori Yanagi, Japanese, b. 1915
Studied at the Tokyo National University of Fine Arts and Music, graduating in 1940. From 1940 to 1942, he worked as an architectural assistant to Charlotte Perriand while she was practising in Japan. In 1951, Yanagi won first prize in the inaugural 'Japanese Competition for Industrial Design' and in the following year he founded the Yanagi Industrial Design Institute, of which he is still the director. In 1977, he was appointed director of the Japan Folk Crafts Museum, Tokyo. His work, such as the Butterfly stool of 1956, represents a synthesis of traditional Japanese craftsmanship and the ideals of the Modern Movement.

Marco Zanuso, Italian, b. 1916
Studied architecture at the Politecnico di Milano, graduating in 1939. In 1945, he established his own design office based in Milan. He was a director of *Domus* and from 1947 editor of *Casabella*. His Lady chair (1951) was highly innovative in its use of materials and won a gold medal at the 1951 Milan Triennale. His later Child's chair (1961), designed in collaboration with Richard Sapper, was the first furniture design produced in polyethylene.

Bibliography (Editions given are those consulted by the authors)

Aloi, R., *Esempi di Arredamento Moderno di Tutto il Mondo: Tavoli, Tavolini, Carrelli*, Ulrico Hoepli Editore, Milan 1955
— *Mobili Tipo*, Ulrico Hoepli Editore, Milan 1956
— *Esempi di Arredamento Moderno di Tutto il Mondo: Tavoli, Tavolini, Carrelli*, Ulrico Hoepli Editore, Milan 1957
— *Esempi di Arredamento Moderno di Tutto il Mondo: Sedie, Poltrone, Divani*, Ulrico Hoepli Editore, Milan 1957
— *L'Arredamento Moderno*, Ulrico Hoepli Editore, Milan 1964
Amic, Y., *Intérieurs: Le mobilier français 1945–1964*, Editions du Regard, Paris 1983
Anargyros, S., *Intérieurs: Le mobilier français 1980 . . .*, Editions du Regard, Paris 1983
— *Le Style Des Années 80: Architecture, Decoration, Design*, Editions Rivages, Paris 1986
Anscombe, I. and C. Gere, *Arts and Crafts in Britain and America*, Academy Editions, London 1978
Bangert, A., *Italian Furniture Design: Ideas Styles Movements*, Bangert Verlag/Bangert Publications, Munich 1988
Baroni, D., *Gerrit Thomas Rietveld Furniture*, Academy Editions, London 1978
Bayley, S. (ed.), *The Conran Directory of Design*, Conran Octopus Ltd, London 1985
Baynes, K. and K., *Gordon Russell*, The Design Council, London 1981
Billcliffe, R., *Charles Rennie Mackintosh: The Complete Furniture, Furniture Drawings & Interior Designs*, John Murray, London 1979
Bony, A., *Les Années 50*, Editions du Regard, Paris 1982
— *Les Années 60*, Editions du Regard, Paris 1983
Branzi, A., *The Hot House: Italian New Wave Design*, Thames and Hudson, London 1984
Branzi, A. and M. De Lucchi, *Il Design Italiano Degli Anni'50*, Ricerche Design Editrice, Milan 1985
Brino, G., *Carlo Mollino: Architecture as Autobiography*, Thames and Hudson, London 1987
Brunhammer, Y., *Les Styles des Années 30 à 50*, Baschet & Cie, Paris 1987

Bure, G. de, *Intérieurs: Le mobilier français 1965–1979*, Editions du Regard, Paris 1983
Caplan, R., *The Design of Herman Miller*, Whitney Lilbrary of Design, New York 1976
Collins, M., *Towards Post-Modernism: Design Since 1851*, British Museum Publications, London 1987
Collins, M. and A. Papadakis, *Post-Modern Design*, Academy Editions, London 1989
Conway, H., *Ernest Race*, The Design Council, London 1982
DiNoto, A., *Art Plastic: Designed for Living*, Abbeville Press, New York 1984
Dormer, P., *The New Furniture: Trends and Traditions*, Thames and Hudson, London 1987
— *The Meanings of Modern Design: Towards the Twenty-First Century*, Thames and Hudson, London 1990
Drake, N., *The Fifties in Vogue*, Condé Nast Publications, London 1987
Drexler, A., *Charles Eames Furniture from the Design Collection*, The Museum of Modern Art, New York 1973
Favata, I., *Joe Colombo and Italian Design of the Sixties*, Thames and Hudson, London 1988
Fehrman, C. and K., *Postwar Interior Design: 1945–1960*, Van Nostrand Reinhold, New York 1987
Forty, A., *Objects of Desire: Design and Society 1750–1980*, Thames and Hudson, London 1986
Frampton, K., *Modern Architecture: A Critical History*, Thames and Hudson, London 1980
Frey, G., *Schweizer Möbeldesign 1927–1984*, Bentili Verlag Bern, Lausanne 1986
Friedman, M., *De Stijl, 1917–1931: Visions of Utopia*, Phaidon, Oxford 1982
Garner, P., *Phaidon Encyclopedia of Decorative Arts 1890–1940*, Phaidon, Oxford 1978
— *Contemporary Decorative Arts: From 1940 to the Present Day*, New Burlington Books, London 1980
— *20th-Century Furniture*, Phaidon, Oxford 1980
Gramigna, G., *1950/1980 Repertory: Pictures and Ideas Regarding the History of Italian Furniture*, Arnoldo Mondadori Editore,

Milan 1985
Greenburg, C., *Mid-Century Modern: Furniture of the 1950s*, Thames and Hudson, London 1985
Grow, L., *Modern Style: A Catalogue of Contemporary Design*, The Main Street Press, New Jersey 1985
Habegger, J. and J.H. Osman, *Sourcebook of Modern Furniture*, Van Nostrand Reinhold, New York 1989
Hamilton, R., *Collected Words*, Thames and Hudson, London 1982
Harling, R., *Modern Furniture and Decoration*, House & Garden/ Condé Nast Publications, London 1971
Harris, J., S. Hyde and G. Smith, *1966 and All That: Design and Consumerism in Britain 1960–1969*, Trefoil Books, London 1986
Hayward, H., *World Furniture*, Hamlyn, Feltham 1965
Heisinger, K. and G. Marcus, *Design Since 1945*, Thames and Hudson, London 1983
Horn, R., *Fifties Style: Then & Now*, Columbus Books, Kent 1985
Huygen, F., *British Design: Image and Identity*, Thames and Hudson, London 1989
Kallir, J., *Viennese Design and the Wiener Werksaïtte*, Thames and Hudson, London 1986
Katz, S., *Classic Plastics: From Bakelite to High-Tech*, Thames and Hudson, London 1984
— *Plastics: Designs and Materials*, Studio Vista, London 1987
Klein, D. and M. Bishop, *Decorative Art 1880–1980*, Phaidon/Christie's, Oxford 1986
Larrabee, E. and M. Vignelli, *Knoll Design*, Harry N. Abrams, New York 1981
Loewy, R., *Industrial Design*, Fourth Estate, London 1979
Lucie-Smith, E., *Furniture: A Concise History*, Thames and Hudson, London 1979
— *A History of Industrial Design*, Phaidon, Oxford 1983
Lyall, S., *Hille: 75 Years of British Furniture*, Elron Press/Victoria and Albert Museum, London 1981
Maassen, L., *Herman Miller Magazine*, Herman Miller Inc., Zeeland, Michigan 1989
MacCarthy, F., *British Design Since 1880: A Visual History*, Lund Humphries, London 1982

Mastropietro, M., *An Industry for Design: The Research, Designers and Corporate Image of B & B Italia*, Edizioni Lybra Immagine s.n.c., Milan 1982

Morgan, A.L., *Contemporary Designers*, St James Press, London 1985

Naylor, G., *The Bauhaus Reassessed*, Herbert Press, London 1985

Nelson, G., *Living Spaces*, Whitney Publications, New York 1952

— *George Nelson Design*, Whitney Library of Design, New York 1979

Nelson, G. and H. Wright, *Tomorrow's House: A Complete Guide for the Home Builder*, Simon & Schuster, New York 1946

Neuhart, J., M. Neuhart and R. Eames, *Eames Design: The Work of the Office of Charles and Ray Eames*, Harry N. Abrams, New York 1989

Ostergard, D.E., *Mackintosh to Mollino: Fifty Years of Chair Design*, Barry Friedman, New York 1984

Page, M., *Furniture Designed by Architects*, Whitney Library of Design, New York 1980

Payne, C., *Sotheby's Concise Encyclopedia of Furniture*, Conran Octopus, London 1989

Pevsner, N., *The Sources of Modern Architecture and Design*, Thames and Hudson, London 1968

— *Pioneers of Modern Design*, Penguin, Harmondsworth 1986

Ponti, L.L., *Gio Ponti: The Complete Work 1923–1978*, Thames and Hudson, London 1990

Renaud, P., *Starck: Mobilier*, Michel Aveline Editeur, Marseille 1987

Russell, F., P. Garner and J. Read, *A Century of Chair Design*, Academy Editions, London 1980

Rutherford, J., *Art Nouveau, Art Deco & The Thirties: The Furniture Collections at Brighton Museum*, The Royal Pavilion, Art Gallery and Museums, Brighton 1983

Schildt, G., *Alvar Aalto: The Decisive Years*, Rizzoli, New York 1986

Schweiger, W.J., *Wiener Werkstätte: Design in Vienna 1903–1932*, Thames and Hudson, London 1984

Sembach, K.J., *Contemporary Furniture: An International Review of Modern Furniture 1950 to the Present*, The Design Council, London 1982

Sparke, P., *Furniture: Twentieth-Century Design*, E.P. Dutton, New York 1986

— *Italian Design: 1870 to the Present*, Thames and Hudson, London 1988

— *The Plastics Age: From Modernity to Post-Modernity*, Victoria and Albert Museum, London 1990

Sparke, P., F. Hodges, A. Stone and E. Coad, *Design Source Book: A Visual Reference from 1850 to the Present Day*, Macdonald Orbis, London 1986

Stewart Johnson, J., *Eileen Gray: Designer*, Museum of Modern Art, New York 1979

Stimpson, M., *Modern Furniture Classics*, The Architectural Press, London 1987

Sudjic, D., *From Matt Black to Memphis and Back Again*, Architecture Design and Technology Press, London 1989

— *Ron Arad: Restless Furniture*, Fourth Estate/Wordsearch, London 1989

Taragin, D., E.S. Cooke and J. Giovanni, *Furniture by Wendell Castle*, Hudson Hills Press, New York 1989

Thackara, J., J. Stuart and P. Dormer, *New British Design*, Thames and Hudson, London 1986

Vanlaethem, F., *Gaetano Pesce: Architecture, Design, Art*, Thames and Hudson, London 1989

Vercelloni, V., *The Adventure of Design: Gavina*, Editoriale Jaca Book spa, Milan 1987

Wilk, C., *Marcel Breuer: Furniture & Interiors*, Museum of Modern Art, New York 1981

Whiteley, N., *Pop Design: Modernism to Mod*, The Design Council, London 1987

Wright, F.L., *An Autobiography*, Faber & Faber, London 1945

Young, D. and B., *Furniture in Britain Today*, Editore Salto, Milan 1964

Exhibition catalogues

Alvar Aalto: Furniture and Glass, The Museum of Modern Art, New York 1984

Les Années 50, Centre Georges Pompidou, Paris 1988

The Architecture of Frank Gehry, Walker Art Gallery, Minneapolis/Rizzoli, New York, 1986

Avant Première: Contemporary French Furniture, Victoria and Albert Museum/Editions Eprouve, London 1988

Bent Wood and Metal Furniture: 1850–1946, American Federation of Arts, New York 1987

Brani di storia dell'arredo (1880–1980), Museo dell'arredo contemporaneo/Edizioni Essegi, Ravenna 1988

British Art & Design 1900–1960, Victoria and Albert Museum, London 1983

Carlo Mollino Cronaca, Galeria Fulvio Ferrari/Stamperia Artistica Nationale Editrice, Turin 1985

Classic Plastic, Fischer Fine Art Limited, London 1989

Design Français 1960–1990: Trois Decennies, APCI/Editions du Centre Pompidou, Paris 1988

Design im 20. Jahrhundert, Museum für Angewandte Kunst, Cologne

Design in America: The Cranbrook Vision 1925–1950, The Detroit Institute of Arts and The Metropolitan Museum of Art, New York 1983

Gerrit Rietveld: A Centenary Exhibition, Barry Friedman Gallery, New York 1988

High Styles: Twentieth-Century American Design, Whitney Museum/Summit Books, New York 1985

Isamu Noguchi: Space of Akari and Stone, Seibu Museum of Art/Chronicle Books, San Francisco 1985

Italy: The New Domestic Landscape, Museum of Modern Art, New York 1972

Jean Prouvé: Mobilier 1924–1953, Galerie Down-Town and Galerie Touchaleaume, Paris 1987

The Modern Chair: Twentieth-Century British Chair Design, Institute of Contemporary Arts, London 1988

Modern Chairs 1918–1970, Whitechapel Art Gallery/Lund Humphries, London 1970

Ron Arad, Vitra Design Museum, Weil am Rhein 1990

Shape and Environment: Furniture by American Architects, Whitney Museum of American Art, New York 1982

Sottsass Associates, Rizzoli International Publications, New York 1988

Svensk Form: A Conference about Swedish Design, The Design Council, 1981

Index

188

Acknowledgments

We would like to thank Anita Archer for her considerable assistance throughout this project, and numerous designers including Ron Arad, Fred Baier, Wendell Castle, Nigel Coates, Tom Dixon, André Dubreuil, Paul Goldman, Vladimir Kagan, Douglas Kelley, Danny Lane, John Makepeace, Peter Murdoch, and Floris Van den Broecke. We would also like to acknowledge the many galleries, museums, manufacturers, photographers and collectors who have supplied archival information and photography including Arflex, the Barry Friedman Gallery, Christina and Bruno Bischofberger, the Brooklyn Museum, Alan Carter, Cassina, Fifty/50, the Fred Hoffmann Gallery, Fritz Hansen, Peter Hodsoll, Galerie Neotu, Galerie Yves Gastou, Herman Miller, Hille, Ikon, Kartell, Knoll International, Memphis, the Noguchi Foundation, Oscar Woollens, Nick Pace, Poltronova, Rosenthal, SCP, Stendig, Studio Alchymia, Themes & Variations, 20th Century, the Victoria and Albert Museum, Vitra, the Whitechapel Art Gallery, and Zeev Aram. We would like to express our gratitude to our parents for their guidance and constant support.

Lastly, we would like to thank Paul Chave for his wonderful photography. Paul has won numerous awards for his designs for album covers, posters and advertisements and won the coveted 'Times Photographer of the Year Award' in 1986. From his Covent Garden studio he now specializes in the photography of architecture, furniture and still life.

Sources of illustrations

Colour plate numbers are given in roman type; page numbers for black-and-white illustrations are given in *italic*, with the following directionals: *L* (Left), *R* (Right), *T* (Top), *B* (Bottom), *M* (Middle)

A.D. Decorative Arts 3; Arconas 83; Arflex 12, 28, 29, 30, 31; Artery 37; B & B Italia 80, 81; F. Baier 137; Barry Friedman 22, 49; Blueprint 122; Branson Coates Architecture 125; Brooklyn Museum 21; Cadsana 32; Cassina 98, 107, 108, 110, 5, 9, 53, *80(L)*; Chicago Institute of Art *14*; Christie, Manson & Woods *11(B)*; Dixon PID 135; Driade 127; A. Dubreuil 128; Dux International *13(M)*; Fiell – Paul Chave 2, 4, 5, 14, 16, 17, 18, 19, 24, 26, 33, 34, 42, 46, 50, 53, 54, 56, 58, 59, 63, 64, 65, 66, 68, 71, 72, 79, 86, 91, 92, 101, 111, 136, *144*, *12(T)*, *13(B)*, *50(B)*, *80(R)*, *86*, *87*, *113(R)*, *144*, *151*; Fiell – Peter Hodsoll 1, 3, 15, 36, 38, 43, 45 (we are grateful to Lesley Jackson of Manchester City Art Galleries for information concerning this piece), 47, 52, 67, 90, 134, 138, *1*, *6(L)*, *15*, *48(R)*, *51*, *52*, *117*; Fifty/50 11, 13, 27, 39, *20*; Fred Hoffmann Gallery *4(R)*; Fritz Hansen 48, 51, 55, 57; Galerie Bischofberger 6, 7, 8, 9, 22, 35, 44, *4(L)*, *17(R)*; Galerie Neotu 121, 139, 140, 141, 142, 143; Galerie Yves Gastou 49; Herman Miller *16(R)*, *19*; Hille 76, 84, 103, *11*, *48(L)*, *83(T)*, *83(B)*; Johannes Hansens Mobelsnedkeri 10, 20, 23; Kartell 74; Knoll International 33, 60, 61, 69, 77, 78, 97, 118, 120, *10(B)*; D. Lane 123 (K. Summers), 129 (I. McKinnell), 130 (F. Italia), 132 (R. Foster); J. Makepeace 124, *119*, *148*; Memphis 112, 113, 114, 115, 116, *147*; OMK 99; One Off Ltd 133; Poltronova 73, 82, 87, 117; Race Furniture 5, *50(T)*; Rosenthal 93, *116*; SCP *149*; Stendig 85, 88, 89, *70*; Studio Alchymia 104, 105, 106, *118*; Tecno 25, 41; Themes & Variations 96; 20th Century 23; F. Van den Broecke 94, 100, 102; Victoria and Albert Museum *6(R)*, *7(L)*, *7(R)*, *10(T)*, *11(T)*, *12(B)*, *13(T)*; Vitra 40, 109, 126, 131, *17(L)*, *145(L)*, *145(R)*; Whitechapel Art Gallery *16(L)*, *81*, *85*; Zanotta 75, 95, 119, *113(L)*, *115*; Zon International 62.